MW00910266

NOVELL NetWare Troubleshooting:

THE POCKET REFERENCE

Robert Scarola

Osborne **McGraw-Hill**

Berkeley New York St. Louis San Francisco
Auckland Bogotá Hamburg London Madrid
Mexico City Milan Montreal New Delhi Panama City
Paris São Paulo Singapore Sydney
Tokyo Toronto

Osborne **McGraw-Hill**
2600 Tenth Street
Berkeley, California 94710
U.S.A.

Osborne **McGraw-Hill** offers software for sale. For information on software, translations, or book distributors outside of the U.S.A., please write to Osborne **McGraw-Hill** at the above address.

NOVELL NetWare Troubleshooting: The Pocket Reference

Publisher: Kenna S. Wood
Acquisitions Editor: Frances Stack
Associate Editor: Jill Pisoni
Project Editor: Madhu Prasher
Copy Editor: Dusty Bernard
Proofreading Coordinator: Erica Spaberg
Proofreaders: Colleen Paretty, Pat Mannion
Indexer: Valerie Robbins
Book Designers: Michelle Salinaro, Stefany Otis
Typesetting: Helena Charm, Michelle Salinaro, Peter Hancik
Cover Design: Mason Fong

234567890 DOC 998765432

ISBN 0-07-881765-X

This book is lovingly dedicated to Nancy, my wife and life partner, who makes it all possible; and to my two sons, Russell and Ben, growing into the computer age. Their patience as a family with the weekend and evening time I've taken to write this book has been a true measure of their love for me. And I deeply appreciate it.

CONTENTS

Acknowledgments

First, I owe an immeasurable debt of gratitude to Leigh Yafa, who retyped and reformatted every page of this manuscript for me, often more than once. Without Leigh's generous assistance, I simply would not have been able to complete this book.

I also wish to thank all the people I have met over the years in the computer networking world who have inspired and assisted me as I established my company, Computer Access and Training Services, Inc.—particularly, Roy Manalastas, who has always been there with good advice and excellent hardware; and Gregg Ritchie, my cabling guru, who has never failed to "make it work." I owe special thanks as well to my incredibly supportive and hardworking staff, Brent Hamblin, Bruce Farrell, Mark Cordova, and Steve Ingraham, fellow technicians and troubleshooters who daily bring real solutions to our clients in the complex world of network computing.

Next, I wish to thank the editorial staff at Osborne/McGraw-Hill for all their hard work and attention to detail throughout the writing and publication process. I am especially grateful to Frances Stack, Acquisitions Editor, who involved me in this project in the first place and provided throughout the writing and editing stages extremely helpful insights into the structure and perspective that I believe make this book so uniquely useful.

Finally, I owe every engineer and programmer at NOVELL a debt of gratitude for producing a superb networking product, NOVELL NetWare. Any errors or omissions in this book having to do with NOVELL are entirely my responsibility. The outstanding reliability and value of NetWare as a network operating system is entirely due to the diligence and competence of the people at NOVELL.

—*Robert Scarola*

Introduction

I have written *NOVELL NetWare Troubleshooting: The Pocket Reference* to combine brevity and ease of use with technical accuracy so you can reach into your pocket rather than search your bookshelves for answers to common NetWare problems. I want you to have a clear, concise, straightforward reference that is focused specifically on the problems you are most likely to experience on your NetWare local area network (LAN), a reference that provides the solution to each problem described in the text immediately after you understand why the problem has occurred. My goal is simple: to help you fix the problem and get back to the work the LAN is supporting, rather than to have to constantly work to support the LAN.

To assist your troubleshooting as much as possible, I have organized this book as a modular guide. Chapter 1, "System Management," presents the problems that occur during system management of an existing LAN, since these are the most frequent daily problems faced by a network administrator. Chapter 2, "Printing," moves to an area that often requires the most ongoing maintenance. Chapter 3, "The File Server," deals with the file server and the core operating system, NetWare, which must work properly at all times for the LAN to remain functional and operational. These first three chapters are thus devoted to keeping your present LAN working effectively. The last three chapters then focus on LAN problems related to change and expansion. Chapter 4, "Workstation Bootup and NetWare Shell Issues," focuses on DOS, NetWare shell, OS/2, Windows 3.0, and Macintosh problems. Chapter 5, "Workstation Hardware," concentrates on workstation hardware configuration and implementation. And finally, Chapter 6, "Cabling," centers on the critical web that seems to grow with a life and purpose of its own.

This modular structure is designed to help you quickly solve commonly experienced problems and errors that can make local area network life frustrating for the user or the system administrator working in the NOVELL NetWare 2.X environment.

Throughout this book it is assumed you have full supervisor privileges on the network so that when problems occur, you have the ability to access all areas of the network and to make any changes required. However, since you will often be asked to fix problems that develop because users do not have supervisor privileges, user types of problems are also addressed in this text. Therefore, even though as supervisor you may not experience the indicated problems, you will understand the needs of the users who do.

Those of you who are relative newcomers to NOVELL NetWare may need to consult other sources when a solution to a problem is indicated. For that reason, you will find throughout this pocket reference appropriate guides to point you in the right direction for further documentation. For you "old-timers" who have grown with NetWare over this past decade, such guides may not be necessary. However, even veterans of NetWare version 2.1X will find many of the changes in the installation and execution of NetWare version 2.2 significant enough that the exact implementation of some procedures may require a more complete reference book that includes, for instance, detailed procedures for installing a NetWare 2.2 file server. You are pointed to those documents at appropriate times in the text.

You will find this book the most valuable, easiest-to-use, and most convenient troubleshooting tool in your NetWare library: a book small enough to carry with you, yet good enough that you can confidently turn to it as your first line of defense, even when your "file server cannot be found."

1

System Management

Skilled system management of a NetWare 2.X LAN requires
attention to detail. You must carefully plan user login
restrictions, overall network volume and directory
structures, and trustee rights and file attribute
assignments. You must also be prepared to deal with the
vagaries of application program installations and upgrades,
login script customization, and menu setups.

To assist you through the maze of NetWare error message
interpretation, NOVELL provides in 2.2 NetWare the last
325 pages of the "Installing and Maintaining the Network"
manual and in 2.1X NetWare, the "NetWare System
Messages" manual. This manual is organized into three
sections—"Command Line Utilities," "Streaming Tape
Backup/Restore," and "NetWare v2.0a/Shell." In each of
these sections, the error messages are then organized
alphabetically.

In addition, both NetWare 2.1X and NetWare 2.2 offer
on-line help screens and tutorials that you can access from
your DOS prompt on the network by using the command
HELP. If you type **help** on a 2.1X network and it does not
work, it is probably because the 2.1X HELP files were not
installed. These files must be installed separately in the
PUBLIC directory after the file server installation is
completed, and sometimes the NetWare installer forgets to
copy these extra disks onto the file server. (The 2.2 HELP
files are automatically installed on the file server during the
operating system installation process.)

Finally, you should be familiar with and have ready access
to the NetWare 2.1X "Users Guide," "Supervisor's Guide,"
"Command Line Utilities," and "Menu Utilities" manuals

and the NetWare 2.2 "Getting Started" and "Using the Network" manuals. These manuals provide additional guidelines for, and examples of, correct NetWare command usage and syntax. You should be especially familiar with the NetWare menu utilities SYSCON, FCONSOLE, PCONSOLE, and FILER; the NetWare command-line utilities MAP, NDIR, CHKVOL, and FLAG; and LOGIN SCRIPT commands, variables, and syntax rules. These NetWare programs and features are heavily utilized during NetWare system administration.

Together, the NetWare manuals and infobases contain thousands of error messages, many of which are rarely seen. This chapter narrows the focus to the most commonly experienced system-management types of errors. Where it is appropriate, brief command sequences for fixing those errors are included.

Login

After the user gains access to a login prompt such as F:\LOGIN, the user can type the command LOGIN followed by a space, the name of the file server, a slash or backslash (unlike DOS, NetWare will accept either one), and their assigned user name. Their name appears as the user types. The user is then usually prompted for a password. For security reasons, the password does not appear as the user types. If the user types either the name or the password incorrectly, NetWare does not permit the user to log in to a file server.

Symptom

An "Access to server denied," "Access to server denied and you have been logged out," "Failed to attach the server," or "File server name unknown" error message appears on the workstation monitor.

Probable Cause

The user mistyped their login name or password or, on a multiserver network, the user tried to log in to a file server on which he or she does not have any rights.

Solution

Tell the user to carefully retype their assigned login name and password. In a multiserver environment, have the user type the full path to the file server as well. For example:

F:\LOGIN login servername\username

Symptom

The error message "No connection found to specified server," "Not logged into server," or "No connection to server" appears.

Probable Cause

The user tried to execute a command on a file server to which the user is not logged in or attached.

Solution

Tell the user to attempt to log in or attach to the file server again. If the user logs in, he or she will be logged out from their default file server and the connection to it (and to any other servers) will be lost. If the user attaches to a file server, he or she will retain all current connections and be able to execute commands on that file server. To attach to a file server, the user types attach servername. The user is then prompted for a login name and password. Remember that a user cannot be attached to more than eight file servers at a time.

Even if the user cannot log in to the file server the user is attached to, from its F:\LOGIN directory the user should be able to type the command SLIST (for ServerList) and see a list of available file servers in order to log in to the correct one. If the user cannot see the servername with SLIST, the file server is either disconnected from the workstation (see Chapter 5, "Workstation Hardware," and Chapter 6, "Cabling") or it is down or has failed (see Chapter 3, "The File Server").

➤   *Tech tip: Do not be confused if a user says he or she is attached to a file server but not able to log in to it. A user can access any file server's LOGIN directory, but unless the user has a valid user name and password on that server, the user will not be able to log in to it. And NetWare will attach the user to the first available file server unless the workstation or boot disk has a "preferred server=" statement in its SHELL.CFG file (see Chapter 4, "Workstation Bootup and NetWare Shell Issues").*

Symptom

The error message "No response from given server" or "Server is unknown at this time" appears when the user tries to log in from one file server to another.

Probable Cause

The file server lost power or was shut off before the DOWN command was issued or the workstation has lost physical connection between the two file servers.

Solution

Check the designated file server and power it up again if it has shut down, or check relevant network boards, connections, and cabling. (See Chapter 4, "Workstation Bootup and NetWare Shell Issues," Chapter 5, "Workstation

Hardware," and Chapter 6, "Cabling," for problems related specifically to network board connections and cabling.)

➤ *Tech tip:* *If the file server is not accessible but is still powered on, type* **down** *at the file server's console keyboard before you shut the power off. If nothing appears on the file server monitor as you type, write down any error messages before you power down the file server. Then look in the index in this reference guide for that error message or read Chapter 3, "The File Server," before proceeding.*

Symptom

The error message "Attempting to attach to (or login to) server (servername)" after your "account balance has dropped below the minimum," when you are "without an account balance," or when your "account has expired or been disabled by the supervisor" appears.

Probable Cause

The account balance minimum for that user has been exceeded or was not established by the network supervisor, or the account has expired or been disabled by the network supervisor.

Solution

Log in as supervisor or as a user with supervisor rights to re-enable the account. Use the SYSCON menu utility. Type **syscon**. Then choose User Information, *(username)*, Account Restrictions, or Account Balance to make these changes.

Symptom

An "Attempting to attach to (or login to) server (servername)" during an "unauthorized time period," "simultaneously on too many workstations," or from "an unapproved station" error message appears.

Probable Cause

The network supervisor has limited the login times, the number of stations the user can concurrently log in on, or the station address the user can log in from.

Solution

Log in with supervisor privileges to change these limitations. Use the SYSCON menu utility. Type syscon. Choose User Information, (*username*), Account Restrictions to change the times the user can log in and the number of stations the user can log in on. Choose User Information, (*username*), Station Restrictions to change the station address the user can log in from.

Symptom

An "Intruder detection lockout has disabled this account" error message appears.

Probable Cause

The user did not type the correct password within the allowed number of logins or someone else has tried to access the user account and intruder detection has been activated on the file server to prevent intruder access.

Solution

Either someone has tried to illegally access the file server or the user mistyped his or her password. Have the user retype their password correctly. (If the user simply has trouble remembering their password or typing it, have them change it by typing setpass.) If someone disables the supervisor account by trying to log in with the name Supervisor but with incorrect passwords, the supervisor account can be re-enabled by typing enable login at the file server console. This *only* works for the login name Supervisor.

Symptom

The user receives the error message "Password has expired and grace login period has also expired."

Probable Cause

The user's password and grace login set up by the supervisor have expired and the account is locked.

Solution

Assign the user a new password.

Symptom

The error "Memory allocation table full" appears when the user attempts to log in.

Probable Cause

The workstation does not have enough memory available to run the LOGIN command.

Solution

Reboot the workstation to clear out any TSRs and try again. If the problem persists, remove any TSRs loading from the AUTOEXEC.BAT file and try again. If the user still has a problem, load the shell into high memory or add more memory (see Chapter 4, "Workstation Bootup and NetWare Shell Issues").

Structure

The volume level on a file server is identical to the root directory level on a local hard disk. Beneath it, you create directories and subdirectories to meet the particular

program and data storage requirements of the network.
Drive mappings are then used to "point to" those
directories and subdirectories.

Problems develop when the volume becomes corrupted
(see Chapter 3, "The File Server"), when the
directory/subdirectory structure is not properly maintained,
when the mappings that point to that structure are
changed or lost, or when the program or data files are
corrupted or deleted.

Symptom

The user attempts to run an application program, utility, or
batch file and receives a "Bad command or file name" error
message.

Probable Cause

The executable file has been deleted or the user mistyped
its name, the proper subdirectory structure has been
modified or removed, or the user lost the search drive
mappings that pointed to the executable program files.

Solution

Use NDIR to look for the files in the appropriate program
directory. For example, at the f:\subdirectory prompt, type
ndir *.com, ndir *.exe, and ndir *.bat to see all the
executable files and batch files. Retype the program file
name correctly. If no executable file exists, reinstall the
program from original disks. If these files do exist, have the
user type map to see if the user has a correct search drive
mapping. If the user does not, use the MAP command to
assign one. For example, use

MAP INS S16:=FS1\SYS:APPS*MYPROG*

if the user's program files are stored in the subdirectory
MYPROG, under the directory APPS, on volume SYS:, on

file server FS1. Include the MAP assignment in your login script to make the change permanent (see the "Login Scripts" section later in this chapter).

➤ *Tech tip:* *Use the map ins s16:= syntax for assigning search drive mappings to avoid overwriting existing search drive mappings. Since there are only 16 search drives available and since search drives must always be numbered sequentially, this syntax automatically uses the next available search drive number for the search assignment. The "ins" guarantees that you will insert this drive mapping and not replace any existing search drive mapping, thus preserving the existing path.*

Also, note that NetWare does not care if you use a / or a \ in its syntax. Any DOS commands used on a network, however, still follow DOS syntax rules.

Symptom

The error message "Illegal search drive specification" or "Network drive specification too high" appears as you use the map command to map search drives or regular drives.

Probable Cause

You either mistyped the syntax for mapping drives or you have exceeded the limit of 16 search drives and 26 regular drives defined at one time.

Solution

Retype the command with the correct syntax. If the problem persists, type `map` and delete any unneeded regular drive or search drive. For example, typing map del k: deletes the regular drive mapping K:; map del s8: deletes search drive 8. Now try to map the new drive again.

Symptom

The user's program runs, but when the user attempts to access the data files, he or she receives a "File not found" error message.

Probable Cause

The files have been deleted, the proper subdirectory structure no longer exists, the user lost the regular drive mappings that point to the data files, or the program will not search the path or insists that data files appear in the same directory as the program.

Solution

Use the NDIR command or the FILER menu utility to look for files in the appropriate data subdirectory. If they exist, have the user type **map** at any prompt to see if they have the correct regular drive mapping. Use the MAP command to assign the correct regular drive mapping by typing

map (*drive letter*):=*fileservername\volumename\ directory path*

Include this statement in the login script to make the change permanent. For example, use

MAP G:=FSI\SYS:DATA\MYFILES

if the data files are stored in the subdirectory MYFILES, under the directory DATA, on volume SYS:, on the file server FSI, and you want to assign the drive letter G: to that subdirectory.

If the files are gone, the SALVAGE utility might recover the deleted files. (SALVAGE does not work on local drives.) However, in 2.X NetWare the user can recover files only if he or she does not log out after deleting them and if they do not subsequently erase any other files. SALVAGE recovers only the last file deleted and should be typed as soon as possible after file deletion in order to work. To use SALVAGE, just have the user type salvage at the DOS prompt of the directory in which the user deleted the files. If the user deleted files from within an application program, have them "shell out" of the application program to the DOS prompt and type salvage. Do not let the user exit from the application program and then use SALVAGE since this usually means they will reaccess the menu system after they exit from their program, which in turn erases the temporary files the menu system created. SALVAGE then unerases only those temporary files and not the data files needed. If the problem persists, check the program reference manual or contact the manufacturer of the program to determine how the program needs to access data.

Symptom

You receive the error message "Unable to get drive mapping" or "Unable to get mapping for drive."

Probable Cause

You tried to map a drive to a file server on an internetwork that has either gone down or is running an older, incompatible version of NetWare.

Solution

Bring the file server back up or upgrade it to a newer version of NetWare (see Chapter 3, "The File Server").

Symptom

A "Directory is not locatable or non-existent," "Invalid directory or drive specification," or "Error mapping drive" error message occurs.

Probable Cause

You attempted to map to a nonexistent directory or the file server has run out of memory space to hold drive mappings.

Solution

Retype the map command or change it in the login script (see the following section on "Login Scripts") to point to the correct directory, or rename the directory with the RENDIR command. If the error persists, log out, reboot the workstation, and try again. If the problem continues, add more RAM at the file server (see Chapter 3, "The File Server") or have other users remove unneeded drive mappings.

➤ *Tech tip: Unlike DOS, NetWare provides the RENDIR command so you can rename directories without having to delete them and re-create them. (Third-party utilities can perform this function for you in DOS.) Type* **rendir oldname newname***. But be careful! NetWare automatically updates this directory name change in the trustee rights assignments. However, login scripts, batch files, and menus must be manually edited by you to reflect the new directory path or you will lose access to the files in those directories.*

Rights

Once users have logged in to the file server, their trustee rights assignments control their access level to programs and data on the network. As supervisor, or a user with supervisor-equivalent privileges, you have all rights in all volumes and directories on a file server. The supervisor has the following rights: Read, Open, Search (in 2.2 NetWare, Open and Search have been combined into Filescan [F] to be consistent with NetWare 3.11 usage), Create, Write, and Delete files, and Modify file attributes (ROSCWDM). He or she also has the Parental (P) right to grant other users rights. Other users and groups are created and assigned access rights to directories and subdirectories by the supervisor.

Rights flow downward through the directory structure unless they are reassigned at a lower level or modified by a directory rights mask. Effective rights in a directory are thus a combination of rights assigned to a user, rights assigned by virtue of a user's membership in groups, and the rights permissions granted by the supervisor through the directory rights mask. In addition, files can be flagged with attributes such as Read Only (RO), Read/Write (RW), Hidden (H), System (SY), Shareable (S), and Non-Shareable (NS). These attributes take precedence over rights granted in a directory. That is, you could be logged in as supervisor and have all rights in a directory, but by itself, that does not change the status of the file attributes. You must exercise your Modify right and reflag the file attributes you wish to change with the FLAG command. (For a complete discussion of rights, see the NetWare 2.2 "Concepts" and "Using the Network" manuals and the NetWare 2.1X "Getting Started and Supervisor's Reference" and "Command Line Utilities" manuals.) Users can find out their rights in any subdirectory by simply typing the command RIGHTS at the subdirectory prompt.

Symptom

The user attempts to run a program and receives a "Bad command or filename" error message, or attempts to access a data file and receives a "File not found" or "You have no rights to copy a file from" error message. However, other users can run the program and access the data files.

Probable Cause

The user has lost the appropriate drive mappings to the program and data file subdirectories (see the section on "Structure" above), or does not have sufficient rights in the directories where the files are stored.

Solution

Log in as supervisor to have the user's effective rights changed in the relevant directories to permit access. The user needs a minimum of Read, Open, and Search rights (ROS) in 2.1X NetWare and Read and Filescan (RF) rights in 2.2 NetWare to run programs and read from files.

Symptom

"Error writing a file," "Error copying a file to," "Error creating a file," or "Access denied" error messages appear when the user attempts to create a file in, copy a file to, or delete a file from a subdirectory.

Probable Cause

The user does not have sufficient rights in the directory to write, create, or delete the file; the user needs to have Write, Create, and Delete (WCD) rights in the subdirectory. Or the file has been marked with a Read Only (RO) or Hidden (H) file attribute.

Solution

Log in as supervisor and assign the user the needed WCD rights. If problems persist, type **ndir** *.* in the subdirectory and check the attributes on the file(s) the user is trying to write, create, or delete. Change the attributes by typing **flag filename n** for "Normal," which is Non-Shareable Read/Write. Grant the user Write, Create, and Delete (WCD) rights in data directories the user will be writing to and flag the files correctly.

If NDIR reveals the file is flagged with a hidden attribute (H), you will need to use the command SHOWFILE to unhide it with NetWare 2.1X before it can be flagged as Normal (the FLAG FILENAME N command will work with NetWare 2.2). Since SHOWFILE is located in the SYSTEM directory, type

f:\system\showfile *filename*

at the directory prompt in order to run SHOWFILE.

➤ *Tech tip:* *File-creation or writing-to-file error messages may also result from the supervisor limiting the disk storage space available to the user on the file server. If the problem persists, have the user type* **chkvol** *at the command-line prompt. If CHKVOL indicates the user has 0 bytes of disk space available, increase the space or delete unneeded files. If the problem affects all users, the file server may be out of storage space entirely, or there may not be any more directory entries left in the file server's directory entry table (DET). You will need to delete files, increase the number of directory entries on the volume, or add more hard disk space to the file server (see Chapter 3, "The File Server").*

Symptom

A "Failed to open file" or "Insufficient rights to create a file" error message occurs when a user tries to create a file, copy to a file, or delete a file.

Probable Cause

The file is currently in use, is waiting in a print queue to be printed (and is therefore held open), or is flagged Read Only (RO), or the user is limited to Read Only rights in the directory.

Solution

If the user has WCD rights in the directory, flag the file Normal (Non-Shareable Read/Write) and have the user try again. Type **flag filename n**. If the flag command also reports an error, the file is being held open. Run PCONSOLE to see if the file is currently in a queue waiting to be printed. You will have to either wait until it prints or delete it from the queue (see Chapter 2, "Printing"). If the file is not in a queue, then it is in use by another user and you will have to wait until it is no longer being accessed.

Login Scripts

There are three types of login scripts on a NetWare file server—default, user, and system. Since these login scripts automate the process of accessing menus, programs, and data on the file server, it is important to understand how they relate to each other.

The default login script is coded into the LOGIN.EXE file stored in the F:\LOGIN directory. This login script sets up critical default search drive mappings to the PUBLIC and DOS subdirectories and regular drive mappings to the root volume directory area. It executes under the following conditions: if neither a system nor user login script exists, or if a system login script exists, no user login script exists, and you do not leave the system login script from an EXIT command.

The system login script sets up global search drive mappings to the PUBLIC and DOS directories and to application directories. It is also used to establish global environmental settings such as the COMSPEC pointer to COMMAND.COM and DOS SET variables, print job routing, home directory drive mappings for all users, and an exit path to a user login script or a menu. Once a system login script is created, it cannot be avoided—not even by the system supervisor. Thus, if the system login script is corrupted or contains errors, it can cause minor to severe network problems for all users. Note that you must be logged in as supervisor or have supervisor-equivalent status on the network to edit the system login script using SYSCON.

The user login script executes if you do not exit from the system login script with the EXIT command. The user login script is used for further customization of any global settings to meet the needs of an individual user. If the user login executes, the default login script does not execute. The user can edit his or her own user login script, but cannot edit any other user login script unless the user has supervisor-equivalent status.

The system and user login scripts are usually edited with SYSCON. However, they are both stored as Read Only text files on the file server and can be edited with a text editor. User login scripts are stored in each user's MAIL directory in a text file called LOGIN. The system login script is contained in a text file called NET$LOG.DAT located in the PUBLIC directory.

Symptom

The system login script runs, but when you type the command MAP, you notice you have double mappings to the PUBLIC, DOS, and root directory areas.

Probable Cause

You did not exit from the system login script with the EXIT command, and you have no user login script. Therefore, the default login script also executed, adding its drive mappings and bumping those that were mapped in the system login script.

Solution

Change the system login script so that you use the EXIT command to exit from it to a menu program, application program, or batch file. Type **syscon**. Then choose Supervisor Options, System Login Script. You might then, for example, type the line **exit "menu main"** at the end of the system login script. In this example, "main" is the name of the menu script file being run by the command program file MENU.COM.

Symptom

The user cannot access the expected menu or program when he or she logs in. Instead, the error message "More than 14 characters given in EXIT target specification" or "Script error, could not interpret line" appears and the user is returned to a DOS prompt.

Probable Cause

The EXIT command in the login script contains a target file name that is more than 14 characters long or that is not enclosed in quotation marks. If the user does not have a user login script, or if other users also receive the error message, then the problem is in the system login script.

Solution

Access the user's user login script. Type **syscon**. Choose User Information, (*username*), Login Script or if the problem affects all users, access the system login script. Type **syscon**. Choose Supervisor Options, System Login Script. Edit the EXIT statement to make sure that no more than 14 characters are contained in the defined target statement that follows the EXIT command and that the target statement is enclosed in quotation marks—for instance, as in the preceding example, you type **exit "menu main"**.

Symptom

The user logs in to the file server and receives the error message "WARNING: due to a serious error in the execution of this program, further initialization cannot be performed." A message indicating the location of the problem in the login script should then follow the warning message.

Probable Cause

A fatal command error occurred in either the system or user login script and further processing terminates. NetWare usually leaves the user logged in to the PUBLIC directory so the user can use SYSCON to correct the indicated error.

Solution

Use SYSCON to access the user's user login script and correct the error. Type `syscon`. Choose User Information, Login Script. Or if the error is in the system login script, type `syscon`. Choose Supervisor Options, System Login Script. Since there are many errors that can cause this warning message to appear, you should write down the error and then consult one of the appropriate NetWare manuals listed at the beginning of this chapter to find the syntax problem in the login script command line and correct it.

➤ *Tech tip: Depending on the severity of the error in the login script, users may find themselves at the F:\LOGIN prompt instead of F:\PUBLIC. Since they have probably lost critical drive mappings to their NetWare utilities, menu, DOS files, and application programs, nothing works. They may in fact believe they are logged out. Have them type* `cd\public`*. If this works, and it should, they still have access to the PUBLIC directory. If this fails, there is a very fatal error in the system login script, the bindery files have been seriously corrupted, or* *passwords have been lost or changed. (See Chapter 3, "The File Server," for solutions to the problems of bindery corruption and inability to log back in to the network.)*

Symptom

The user created a user login script and now receives a "Bad command or file name" or "File not found" error message when he or she tries to access program or data files.

Probable Cause

The regular or search drive mappings created in the user's user login script have taken precedence over the drive mappings in the system login script.

Solution

Place a Remarks (REM) statement in the beginning of each map line in the user's user login script to disable the lines. Log in again as that user. If everything works as before, remove the REM statements one at a time, logging in after each change, until you find the offending lines in the login script. Make sure you type **map** at the command line after each login to check how drive mappings are being altered.

Symptom

The user receives the error message "Drive (driveletter) is used by the following search mapping(s) S:(number). The search mapping(s) will be deleted. Do you still want to change it?" If the user answers "yes," applications, menus, batch files, or utilities may not run.

Probable Cause

A regular or search drive mapping in the user's user login script is about to overwrite an existing search drive mapping in the system login script.

Solution

Have the user type no, and then at the DOS prompt type map. Use the PRINT-SCREEN key on the user's keyboard to print out the existing drive mappings. Type syscon. Choose User List, (*username*), Login Script to access the login script and change the drive mappings in it to avoid conflicts with existing search drive mappings.

Symptom

The user receives a "Bad or missing command interpreter" message when he or she logs in or when the user leaves application programs.

Probable Cause

The user does not have the correct COMSPEC setting or search drive mapping to DOS in the system login script or the search mapping points to a command interpreter from another version of DOS.

Solution

Log in as supervisor and edit the system login script. (See the section on COMMAND.COM in Chapter 4, "Workstation Bootup and NetWare Shell Issues," for a further discussion of this problem and the correct login script syntax to correct the problem.)

Symptom

The user logs in but does not access the expected menu or program. Instead, the user gets an error message "Cannot read include file" and the user is returned to a DOS prompt.

Probable Cause

The INCLUDE command in the login script specifies a file that does not exist, is not in a search path, is not named correctly, or contains incorrect syntax. If the user does not have a user login script or if other users also receive the error message, then the problem exists in the system login script.

Solution

Access the user's login script. Type **syscon**. Choose User Information, (*username*), Login Script. Or if there is no user login script, Choose Syscon, Supervisor Options, System Login Script. Make sure the INCLUDE statement in the login script points to the correct file. For example, the statement

IF MEMBER OF "ACCOUNT" THEN INCLUDE ACCTFILE

first checks to see if the user is a member of the group account. If the user is, it then looks for a file called ACCTFILE and runs the appropriate script commands in that file. If this statement looks correct, make sure the file you want to include is in a directory in a search path. Finally, if the user still receives an error message, use a text editor to check the INCLUDE file for syntax errors. The command syntax you use in this file is exactly the same as it is for user or system login scripts you edit with SYSCON.

➤ *Tech tip:* *The INCLUDE command is a valuable tool for maintaining large numbers of users on a network. It permits text files containing login script command syntax to be "included" and run as part of a SYSCON-created login script. You thus have the advantage of editing one INCLUDE text file, being accessed by multiple users, as the means for changing all of those users' login scripts. The alternative would be to edit each user's login script individually, a much more time-consuming and error-prone task.*

Further Help

Check the NOVELL "Supervisor's Guide" and "Supervisor's Reference" manuals in NetWare 2.1 and the "Using the

Network" manual in NetWare 2.2 for assistance with syntax rules for login script commands.

Symptom

As the user logs in, he or she receives the error message "Unknown LOGIN script command" or "Unrecognizable conditional operator; Remainder of login script ignored."

Probable Cause

The user's user login script or the system login script contains an invalid command, incorrect syntax, or an incorrect conditional line in an IF...THEN statement.

Solution

Type syscon. Choose User Information, Login Script or Supervisor Options, System Login Script. Make sure all commands are typed correctly. For example, you may have typed drive g instead of drive g: or day-of-week instead of day_of_week Make sure you did not omit a key word such as an equals or a then in a conditional statement. Make sure you enclosed constants within quotation marks: day_of_week = "monday", not monday.

Further Help

Again, the NetWare 2.1X "Supervisor's Guide" and "Supervisor's Reference" and the NetWare 2.2 "Using the Network" manual are excellent references for further assistance with login script syntax and IF...THEN statement usage rules.

Symptom

The user accesses an application program, but while using it, suddenly receives an "Out of memory" error message.

Probable Cause

The user is loading a TSR that has taken up too much memory or has been loaded in from a login script or a menu (see Chapter 4, "Workstation Bootup and NetWare Shell Issues"). There is bad RAM or not enough RAM in your workstation (see Chapter 5, "Workstation Hardware"). Or the user is loading your application from a login script using the # symbol instead of from an EXIT command or a menu. If a major application program loads using the # symbol, the login script remains resident while the application program runs. Since the login script uses up about 70K of RAM until you leave it with the EXIT command, this much RAM is no longer available to the application program while it is running.

Solution

Do not load application programs using the # symbol in login scripts. The # symbol is used to load a program and then return to the login script after the program loads to continue running the rest of the script. For example, #SYSTIME executes the NetWare command that synchronizes all workstations to the file server date and time and then returns to the login script. You can safely use the # symbol for commands such as SYSTIME or CAPTURE statements or NetWare utilities, but not for major applications.

➤ *Tech tip: If you need to run a DOS internal command or a batch file using the # symbol, you must precede the command with a COMMAND /C statement. For example, you can type* **#command /c cls** *or* **#command /c run.bat***. This syntax temporarily loads in a new COMMAND.COM for processing the internal DOS command or batch file.*

Application Programs

Since there are almost as many application programs as there are programmers to write them, and since the idiosyncrasies of the programmers are often mirrored in the performance of their programs, it is impossible to categorize error messages generically in this section. However, if you understand the type of program you are dealing with and have an overall sense of how it performs on the network, there is a common troubleshooting methodology you can try with any malfunctioning application program.

There are essentially three types of application programs used on networks. First, there are single-user application programs that are installed on a NetWare file server and can only be accessed by one user at a time, albeit from different workstations.

Then there are application programs designed initially as single-user programs but eventually modified so that, as they evolve, file and record locking, printer spooling, and other network features are added. These programs have enough network capability to be accessed by multiple users at the same time.

Finally, there are those programs designed initially or modified substantially specifically to work on NOVELL networks, to service multiple users, and to take advantage of NetWare's file, database, and print services, as well as other features.

The last type of program is often more well behaved on the network than the first two types and, when there are problems, demonstrates an awareness of NetWare's processes and functions in the error messages it generates. The first two types of programs, on the other hand, often generate misleading error messages when they have problems since they have been coded to perceive errors from a single-computer, rather than a network file server, perspective.

Because of these differences in application program design and evolution, you will often have no choice but to consult each specific application program's manual or call the program manufacturer's technical support hotline for assistance when you troubleshoot a problem. Even then, tracking down the source of the problem and fixing it can be a very hit-and-miss, time-consuming project in which the first step usually is to determine if the error is related to the network or is isolated to the program. However, even this simple determination may be difficult to make with programs that are not very network smart since, as already indicated, the error messages they generate may or may not point to the true cause of the problem.

Because of this kind of wide divergence in how application programs handle network problems, this section is based on a general approach to isolating problems rather than specific error messages.

Symptom

The application program indicates it cannot write to the disk or read from the disk. The error message may appear to indicate severe disk problems such as "Critical error writing to hard disk."

Probable Cause

You may indeed have a failed hard disk if this error is received by more than one user or when you try to run more than one program. Or you may have a failed cable trunk, hub, router, or file server. However, if other programs are functional, or only one user is affected, the problem is likely a network setup issue involving rights or file attributes.

Solution

Type syscon. Choose Group or User Information, Trustee Rights, and make sure all users who need write access to the program's data files have Write, Create, and Delete (WCD) rights in the necessary subdirectories. Next, use the FLAG command to make sure that none of the files being written to are flagged Read Only (RO). Type flag *.* or ndir *.* to check the attributes of the files in the subdirectory. Type flag (filename) srw to flag a file Shareable Read/Write so it can be written to.

Symptom

The application program works intermittently.

Probable Cause

The program files have been corrupted, there are network board or cabling problems, or there is a workstation or file server problem.

Solution

See how widespread the problem is. If the problem is isolated to a single user, make sure the user is using the program properly. Next, check the user's workstation for DOS, Shell, environment, RAM, network board, or cable connector problems (see Chapters 4 through 6). If the problem is more widespread, try reinstalling the program from known good original disks. If the problem persists, check for file server RAM or hard drive problems (see Chapter 3, "The File Server").

Further Help

Call the program manufacturer for technical support.

➤ *Tech tip: If you have enough room on the file server hard disk, one neat trick is to leave the program installed in its current location but to rename the directory it is installed in by using the RENDIR command—for example, RENDIR PROGRAMS NEWPROGS. Then create a new directory on the hard disk, giving it the original program directory name, and install the program from scratch to that new directory. Move data files as well, if necessary, and test the program.*

This procedure invokes NetWare's Hot Fix routine and ensures the program is reinstalled to good block locations on the hard disk. It is possible that the block locations the program is currently installed in have developed bad areas since the installation. If the program works after this reinstallation process, you can go back and delete the old program files. As you write new data to the disk, Hot Fix should now find any corrupted blocks that were being used by those files and lock them out.

Symptom

You are logged on as supervisor and you attempt to install an upgrade to an existing program. The installation program fails and returns an error message indicating there has been a hard disk failure or the hard drive is full.

Probable Cause

You may have a hard disk failure, no room left on the hard disk, or no directory entries left on the hard disk (see Chapter 3, "The File Server"). But first make sure the program files you are trying to upgrade have not simply been left flagged Read Only (RO).

Solution

Flag all the files in the directory containing the application files you are upgrading N for Normal: type **flag** *.* **n.** Then try again to install the upgrade. Remember, just because you are logged in as supervisor does not mean you automatically override file attribute settings. You must change attributes manually.

Symptom

When more than one user attempts to access the application program, it locks up.

Probable Cause

The application program is a single-user program, it is a network program installed incorrectly as a single-user program, or the files were not flagged to be shared by multiple users at the same time.

Solution

If the application program is single-user only, restrict access to it on the network to only those users who need it, and set up access controls so users do not conflict with each other. You may have to set up a use schedule or have users make use of the SEND command to warn each other when they are about to access the program. If it is a network shareable program, check the application program's manual to make sure it was installed correctly for a network. If problems persist, use the FLAG command to make sure the files are flagged Shareable. Type **flag filename sro** or **srw** to flag files Shareable Read Only or Shareable Read/Write.

➤ *Tech tip: Remember, there are legal ramifications to using single-user programs on a network, even if they are used by only one person at a time, and you should be very clear about your right to do so. In addition, if you use the SEND command, remember that it halts all processing at the receiving workstation until a* CTRL-END *key sequence is entered at that workstation. This could cause serious processing delays at workstations users have left unattended.*

Menus

NOVELL offers an excellent menu utility with NetWare. It provides a clean screen mask, the ability to nest submenus, an easy configuration process, and programming flexibility using variables. In order to use this NetWare menu utility, you must first create a script file that contains the correct syntax and ends in the extension .MNU. (If you do not use that extension, you must include the extension name you are using when you call the script file with the NetWare MENU.EXE program.) Next, place this script file in a subdirectory accessible to users, and grant them Read, Open, and Search rights in that subdirectory. Finally, make the script file accessible by using the NetWare MENU.EXE program file. For example, the command-line statement MENU MAIN executes a menu script file named MAIN that ends in the extension .MNU.

There is also a multitude of third-party menus available from a wide range of vendors, each of which provides unique setup and programming features. (Windows is also a type of menu system, but since it is also an operating system environment, it is discussed in Chapter 4, "Workstation Bootup and NetWare Shell Issues.") Common problems that might occur with the NOVELL menu system are described here. Similar problems might occur with third-party menu systems. However, it is difficult to document what form the error messages generated by those systems might take.

Symptom

The user loads an application program and then receives an "Out of memory" error message.

Probable Cause

The NOVELL menu system is a TSR. It remains resident in memory after a program is loaded, taking up about 30K of RAM.

Solution

If the user has a 286 or 386 workstation with 1 megabyte of RAM and is using the newest release of the NetWare workstation shell (version 3.01e or 3.02), you can try to load the shell high by using XMSNET, thus freeing about 30K of RAM. If the workstation has expanded memory available, use EMSNET. If the user has a 386-level machine, you can use third-party products Like Quarterdeck's QEMM to load the shell high. Finally, DOS 5.0 will load the internal DOS commands high, thus freeing more RAM. (See Chapter 4, "Workstation Bootup and NetWare Shell Issues" for details.)

Symptom

The user attempts to load the menu and receives the error message "Cannot create GO0000#.bat. Further program execution is not possible," and the user is left at a DOS prompt.

Probable Cause

The user did not have sufficient rights in the directory from which he or she started the menu to permit creation of the temporary menu startup file. This file tracks the user's particular use of the menu as opposed to all other users. The user must have Read, Open, Search (or Read and Filescan in NetWare 2.2), Write, Create, Delete, and Modify rights (ROSWCDM) in the directory he or she starts the menu from so this file can be created or deleted as necessary by the menu system.

➤ *Tech tip:* *The user should in general start any menu system used with NetWare from a home directory where the user has all rights. Many menu systems write back temporary startup files just as the NOVELL menu system does and will fail or generate errors when the user attempts to load and unload them unless you provide a home directory base. This is also true of Windows 3.0.*

Symptom

The user cannot access a selection on the menu screen. The user receives an error message indicating a syntax problem in the menu script and is returned to the previous menu.

Probable Cause

The menu script file contains a syntax error.

Solution

Edit the menu script file to correct the error. Common errors are

- No % in front of the menu title.
- Menu options are not left justified.
- Menu executables are not indented.
- Submenus are not called correctly.

Further Help

Check your NetWare 2.1X "Menu Utilities" manual and your NetWare 2.2 "Using the Network" manual for guidance in creating menu script files.

Symptom

You attempt to edit the menu script file and receive an "Access denied" error message.

Probable Cause

The menu script file is in use by another user and is therefore an open file; NetWare will not give you access to the file until the file is closed. Or the file is marked Read Only.

Solution

Wait until no one is using the menu system to edit the script file. Or to avoid waiting, copy the menu script file to another file name—for example, type `copy main.mnu main1.mnu`. Edit the newly created file as you wish. When all users are out of the original menu script file, copy your newly created script file back over the original. Make sure you first check to see that the file is flagged Shareable Read/Write.

Symptom

The user exits your application program and is not able to return to the menu. Instead the user is given a "Bad command or file name" error message and returns to a DOS prompt.

Probable Cause

While in the application, the user invoked a command that caused the CD command to execute and change the search drive mapping to the subdirectory where the menu is stored.

Solution

Have the user type `cd\public` or `cd\login` to change into the PUBLIC or LOGIN directory, and then log in to the file server again to reset the drive mappings. To prevent this from occurring on a regular basis, if you are using the new version (3.01e or 3.02) of the NetWare shell (see Chapter 4, "Workstation Bootup and NetWare Shell Issues"), you can use the MAP ROOT command to make it harder for users' search drive mappings to be changed by the CD command.

For example, with the old utilities MAP command, if you had a search drive mapped to a subdirectory called MENU—MAP S8:=SYS:MENU—you would have drive letter S: also mapped to the menu directory since search #8 uses the drive letter S:. If the user accessed that drive by typing S: and then typed cd\data at the S:\MENU> prompt, he or she would remap S: to SYS:DATA and lose the search path to the menu subdirectory. The MAP ROOT command prevents this kind of accidental remapping. When you type map root s8:=sys:menu, the prompt appears as S:\> and the CD\DATA command will not work. Many application programs invoke what is in effect a CD command when users use the directory list feature, thus causing this drive remapping problem to occur.

Symptom

The user attempts to log out from the NetWare menu by using a logout choice on the menu and receives the error messages "Cannot create GO0000#.bat," "Further program execution is not possible," and "Batch file missing." The user is then left at a LOGIN subdirectory prompt.

Probable Cause

Since the menu is a TSR and remains open while the user is in it, the user will get errors when he or she logs out; the menu is still running but cannot find its temporary startup file to close.

Solution

Place an exclamation mark (!) in front of the logout command in the menu script file. This closes the menu file and allows the user to log out properly.

➤ *Tech tip:* *One last warning about the NOVELL menu system. It is a simple matter to access the DOS prompt from any NOVELL menu screen—just press the ESC key on the keyboard, followed by the Y key. Unfortunately, this easy access to the DOS prompt may be highly undesirable, given the complex nature of most networks and the need to secure DOS-level access to the file server hard drive from most users. This unhappy feature has led many system managers to abandon the NOVELL menu system in favor of menu systems that at the very least require a password to exit from them to DOS. Indeed, a secure menu system is a very good way to prevent user-caused problems from occurring on the network. And finally, prevention is truly the best cure of all for network problems.*

➤ *Tech tip:* *To avoid this problem, start the Novell menu system from a batch file which places a logout command immediately after the menu start up command. For example:*

```
START.BAT
echo off
cls
menu main.mnu
logout
```

If this batch file is called from the system or user login script, the user will run the menu in the main.mnu file. But if the user presses the ESC key while in the menu in order to exit to DOS, the batch file will continue its execution and will run the logout command, leaving the user logged out of the network. The user is thus prevented from accessing the DOS prompt while on the network. NOTE: Make sure you exclude the system Supervisor(s) from calling this batch file since the supervisors must always be able to access the DOS prompt as needed.

2
Printing

The major reasons printing problems occur in a network environment are easy to pinpoint. First, printers are very mechanical devices susceptible to problems caused by an accumulation of paper grit and dirt, jamming, or overheating in dot-matrix printers; and toner, paper feed, or roller problems in laserjet printers. Second, you must install and configure printers correctly. You must set DIP switches correctly on dot-matrix printers and menu selections on laserjet printers. You must properly attach cables and connectors. You must correctly install ribbons or toner cartridges. Finally, there are literally hundreds of different manufacturers of dot-matrix and laserjet printers (not to mention such devices as inkjet and paintjet printers and plotters), and each printer has its own unique setup requirements and software drivers. When you throw into this grab bag of printers and software drivers the wide range of formatting possibilities—fonts, type faces, styles, and forms—printing complexities, and consequently printing problems, grow exponentially.

NetWare was designed almost from the beginning to respond to printing complexities by providing the utilities PRINTDEF and PRINTCON to customize network printer drivers and print jobs. And, recently, NOVELL further improved NetWare's ability to deal with increasing demands for printing services. It added to the operating system the capability to set up print servers by using the utility PSERVER.VAP at the file server or PSERVER.EXE at a dedicated workstation. It also added the capability to assign any local workstation printer as a network-shareable remote printer by using the RPRINTER.EXE utility. These capabilities increase the number of potential shared network printers available to users at one file server from 5 at the file server printer ports to 16 at any one of 8 print servers, for a total of 128 printers available on one file server.

Because of this recent change, NetWare now distinguishes core printing services from print server services. Core printing is restricted to the 5 port assignments 2.X NetWare identifies at the file server: LPT1, LPT2, LPT3, COM1, and COM2. You establish core printing during the installation of NetWare at the file server. On the other hand, you install print server printing services by loading the PSERVER Value Added Process (VAP) at the file server or the PSERVER.EXE program at a dedicated workstation.

For a complete description of NetWare's printing installation processes and services, see 2.1X NetWare's "Supervisor's Reference," "Supervisor's Guide," and "Menu Utilities" and the "Print Server Installation" manual that ships separately with the PSERVER utilities disks. For 2.2 NetWare, see the "Print Server" and "Installing and Maintaining the Network" manuals.

This chapter is concerned with problems specifically related to network printing. Therefore, you must first determine if a printer problem is due to electronic or mechanical failure before troubleshooting it as a network-related problem. As just noted, many printer problems can be traced to loose or bad cable connections, bad cables, exceeding the distance limitations for cables, dirt or paper dust clogging the printer, or internal electronic or mechanical failure in the printer or computer. It is beyond the scope of this book to go into detail concerning printer service and repair. However, you can quickly determine whether the problem is a network problem or an electronic or mechanical problem by using the following techniques.

First, turn the printer off, unplug the interface cable from the back of the printer, and then turn the printer on again and run the printer's self-test routine. You run the self-test on most dot-matrix printers by holding down the line feed button as you power on the printer. Laserjets have a self-test selection on their menu screens.

Second, turn off the printer, plug the cable back in, and check to make sure it is tightly connected at the computer end as well as the printer end. Make sure the cable does not exceed 12 to 15 feet in length if it is parallel. Make sure the pin outs are wired properly if it is serial cable; use loop back plugs and a program like CheckIt to test for this problem. If you place the appropriate plug at the end of a cable, you can check the cable as well.

Third, turn on the printer, and then boot the computer the printer is attached to with a DOS disk in drive A. (Of course, if you are testing a file server, you will first need to log out all users, down the file server, and then reboot it.) At the A:\> prompt, type dir > lpt# or dir > com#, where # is the number of the printer port you are testing. This command redirects the output of the DIR command to the designated printer.

The printer should print the drive A directory list. If it does, you know you have a good working printer port, cable, and printer. You may need to send a form feed to the printer or press the form feed switch to get it to output the directory. If the printer does not print, as a last resort you can try replacing the control card that has the printer port on it, if that is possible. (It may not be possible since many computers today have printer ports built in as part of the system board.) If the problem persists, contact your computer manufacturer or vendor for assistance.

Once you have proven the computer can print to the
printer from a DOS prompt, you can proceed to
troubleshoot the problem as a network problem.

Spool, Capture, Jobs, and Queues

NetWare makes use of the command-line utilities
CAPTURE and NPRINT and the console command SPOOL
to properly set up printing. Detailed instructions for using
these commands can be found in the NetWare 2.1X
"Command Line Utilities" and "Console Reference"
manuals and the NetWare 2.2 "Using the Network" manual.

Briefly, you use the SPOOL command at the file server
console to set up default queues that you will print to if
you do not specifically assign a queue by using the
CAPTURE command. You also use SPOOL to assign device
numbers to queues for application programs that can send
print jobs only to numbered devices. Finally, you use the
SPOOL command to provide downward compatibility with
any 2.0a file servers on a multiserver network. (Version 2.0a
of NetWare used the SPOOL command instead of the
CAPTURE command for redirecting local print jobs to
network printers.)

You use the CAPTURE and NPRINT commands in any
version of NetWare above 2.1X to redirect print jobs from
your local printer to a network printer or queue. The
NetWare 2.1X "Command Line Utilities" and 2.2 "Using the
Network" manuals provide a detailed list of the functions of
the various flags that can be used with the CAPTURE and
NPRINT commands.

A queue is simply a numbered subdirectory created in the
SYSTEM directory on the file server by the supervisor or a
user with supervisor-equivalent rights. This subdirectory is

created when you use PCONSOLE to create a queue. When you send a print job to a queue, NetWare creates a temporary file in the queue for that print job. The job is held in the queue until the printer is ready to receive the job, at which time the job is sent for printing. You can find out the numbered names of queues and print jobs by using PCONSOLE. To find out the subdirectory name of a queue, type pconsole. Select Print Queue Information, (*queue name*), Print Queue ID. The object ID number is the name of the subdirectory for that queue in the SYSTEM directory (often with the first one or two zeros dropped). To find out the file name of the print job, type pconsole. Select Print Queue Information, (*queue name*), Current Print Job Entry. You will get a screen that tells you, among other things, the job number for that print job, which is also that print job's file name extension number in the queue.

Symptom

The user sends a job to the printer and receives the error message "Network spooler error—out of space on Volume SYS."

Probable Cause

The print job was deleted while the shell was spooling it, probably because the user is out of space on volume SYS.

Solution

Run CHKVOL or VOLINFO to view space available on volume SYS. Remove unused files if volume SYS: is running out of space.

Symptom

The user receives the error message "An unknown queue error occurred" while trying to print with NPRINT.

Probable Cause

This is not a fatal error and is probably transient.

Solution

Have the user wait a few minutes and try to print the job again.

Symptom

The user receives the error message "No default queue name can be found on server" or "Print queue cannot be serviced by printer because it has been disabled by a queue operator" when the user tries to capture a print job to a queue on the named server.

Probable Cause

The supervisor did not define print queues on the file server, the queues have been lost, or the queue operator or supervisor disabled the queues.

Solution

Have the user send the print job to another file server until you, as supervisor, create queues or reenable the queues to accept print jobs.

➤ *Tech tip:* *Use PCONSOLE to create print queues. Type* **pconsole**. *Select Print Queue Information. Press the* INS *key to create a print queue. If you wish to make the queue available every time a 2.1X server boots up, you must include a statement in the AUTOEXEC.SYS file. Type* **syscon**. *Select Supervisor Options, AUTOEXEC.SYS. Add the line P # add Q (queue name). See the section "Core Printing" later in this chapter for more details.*

Symptom

The user receives the error message "Illegal queue name specification" or "The print queue cannot be found" when he or she uses the CAPTURE or NPRINT command.

Probable Cause

The user either mistyped a queue name or specified a queue not defined on the file server.

Solution

Use PCONSOLE to see which queues are currently defined on the file server and have the user type in the name of the queue correctly. Type pconsole. Select Print Queue Information.

Symptom

The user receives the error message "The specified queues not matched" when the user uses the CAPTURE or NPRINT command.

Probable Cause

The user specified a queue and a printer that are not assigned to each other.

Solution

Tell the user not to specify both a queue and a printer in the CAPTURE or NPRINT command. Specify one or the other. NetWare will automatically assign the queue specified to the correct printer, and the printer to the correct queue.

Symptom

The user receives the error message "The print queue is halted" when he or she tries to send a print job to a queue.

Probable Cause

The print queue operator has flagged the queue so that no new print jobs can be added.

Solution

Type **pconsole**. Select Print Queue Information, (*queue name*), Current Queue Status. Flag the queue to enable it to accept new jobs.

Symptom

The user receives the error message "Server error in retrieving queue ID" when the user attempts to print to a queue.

Probable Cause

The bindery is either locked or corrupted and is therefore inaccessible. The bindery stores the names of users, rights, file servers to which users are attached, and so on.

Solution

Run the utility BINDFIX to repair the bindery files (see Chapter 3, "The File Server").

Symptom

The user sends a print job by using NPRINT, specifies a form name, and receives the error message "The specified form name could not be found" or "Cannot get the information about the specified form."

Probable Cause

The form definition specified exists, but a network error prevented NPRINT from obtaining the form information.

Solution

Have the user wait a few minutes and try again. If the problem persists, use PCONSOLE and PRINTDEF to determine the defined forms.

Further Help

See the NetWare 2.1X "Menu Utilities" and 2.2 "Using the Network" and "Print Server" manuals for detailed instructions.

Symptom

The user receives the error message "The specified print definition could not be found" or "(*job name*) is not a valid PRINTCON job definition" when the user types the name of the print job by using NPRINT or CAPTURE.

Probable Cause

Either the user mistyped the print job name or specified a print job name that has not been defined with PRINTCON for their account.

Solution

Use PRINTCON to see which jobs are currently defined with the user's account. Have the user type the name of the job correctly.

Symptom

You use PRINTDEF to create customized printer devices and receive the error message "There was not enough memory to hold the PrintDef escape sequences."

Probable Cause

The workstation does not have enough memory to hold the escape sequences.

Solution

Add more memory to the workstation or reduce the number of escape sequences in your printer definition.

Symptom

The user uses the CAPTURE or NPRINT command and receive the error message "Printer number expected with the PRINTER select flag."

Probable Cause

The user specified a printer flag option (P=) as part of the NPRINT or CAPTURE command but omitted a printer number.

Solution

Have the user include a printer number (0-4) with the printer flag option. If you do not know which printer numbers exist, on a 2.1X file server or a 2.2 file server with core printing installed, you can go to the file server console and type printer at the colon (:) prompt. This will tell you which printers are running and whether or not they are on line.

➤ *Tech tip: You cannot use a P= flag in the CAPTURE and NPRINT commands with 2.2 NetWare, nor can you type printer at the file server console, if you have installed the PSERVER VAP and told the operating system to not use core printing when you generated the operating system. See the "Core Printing" section later in this chapter.*

Symptom

The user receives the error message "Local printer number (1, 2, or 3) expected," or "Local printer number is invalid."

Probable Cause

The user used the L= flag without a local printer number or with an invalid printer number.

Solution

Have the user specify the printer number 1, 2, or 3 after the L= flag.

Symptom

The user receives the error message "Illegal banner specification," or "Illegal name specification" when he or she uses the CAPTURE or NPRINT command.

Probable Cause

The user used a banner flag without specifying a banner, specified a banner longer than 12 characters, or specified a banner name longer than 12 characters.

Solution

Have the user retype the command using the correct syntax.

Symptom

The user tries to print a file and receives the error message "You have no rights to print from this directory."

Probable Cause

The user tried to print a file located in a directory in which he or she does not have at least Read, Open, and Search rights (in NetWare 2.2, Read and Filescan rights).

Solution

Assign the user at least these rights in this directory (see Chapter 1, "System Management").

Symptom

The user sends a print job and the printer prints out a mix of the user's print job and other users' print jobs.

Probable Cause

The CAPTURE command allows the queue to accept another job for network printing before a job is finished being sent to the queue. It is normal to set the time-out to TI=10 or 15. This means the queue will wait 10 or 15 seconds before accepting another job for printing. However, if the application program "thinks" about part of the print job and then sends it, then "thinks" about the next part and sends it, and so on in small increments, the time-out may run out before the entire job is sent, permitting a job from another user to intermingle with the current job. This can also happen if the print job is very large—for instance, a graphics image—and takes more than the time-out allocated to send the entire job to the queue.

Solution

Increase the amount of time-out time in the CAPTURE statement. For instance, type ti=60 to raise the time-out to 60 seconds. This increases the time the user must wait before print jobs print but prevents mixed-up print jobs.

➤ *Tech tip:* *You may find you must raise the time-out to 200 or more seconds for some application programs. If this slows down printing unacceptably, send such large print jobs to printers that do not share a queue with other users or to a local printer. The user can also print to a file and then send the file to the printer.*

Symptom

The user tries to capture a graphic design print job from his or her application program to a plotter or laserjet. The plotter or laserjet will not print the job at all or prints garbage.

Probable Cause

Many computer-aided design (CAD) type programs such as AutoCAD have difficulty printing correctly through queues to plotters or laserjets. These programs require a direct "handshaking" response back and forth from the plotter or laserjet. Since sending a print job to a queue does not provide such a response, the job fails to print correctly.

Solution

Use the application program's internal command that allows you to save a print job as a file. Then, exit from the program and use either the DOS COPY command or the NetWare NPRINT command to send the job to the printer. For example, type

```
copy /b plotter.txt lpt1
```

This command copies the file in binary form (/b), since it is a graphics file, to the printer identified as LPT1. Or type

```
nprint plotter.txt q=printq0 nb nff nt
```

This command sends the file to printq0, with no banner, no form feed, and no tabs. The no tabs is important because it sends the file as a byte stream rather than as text so it can be printed out as a graphics file.

Symptom

The printer will not print the print job even though the application program reports the job was sent. You test the printer by using the procedure described at the beginning of this chapter, and the job still will not print. You may receive the error message "The print queue is full."

Probable Cause

An improperly configured print job has been sent to the printer. In other words, the user sent a job from the application program to the printer with the wrong printer device driver selected for the job. For example, the printer is a laserjet but the print job is expecting to find an IBM Proprinter. As a result, the job remains in the queue but cannot print. Other jobs may have stacked up in the queue behind it to the limit of 100 jobs. (Note that a slow printer—especially a dot-matrix—and a lot of small print jobs sent to the queue can give the same indications. For example, Microsoft Word allows you to highlight as many files in a directory as required and print them one after another with no user intervention.)

Solution

You must use PCONSOLE to access the queue and delete the improperly configured job. Then return to the application program and select the correct printer driver for the printer being used. If the problem is due to a slow dot-matrix printer, make sure the first job in the queue is active and printing. You will then have to simply wait for the jobs to be processed. The ultimate solution, of course, is to buy a faster printer.

➤ *Tech tip: No matter what you do, the user will not be able to print until you delete the improperly configured job stuck in the queue. You can turn the printer off, down the file server, and reboot, and the user will still not be able to print. Remember, as the user's frustration level grows, their print job is now a file in a subdirectory on the file server. It does not go away when power to the file server or the printer is turned off. The job simply waits until NetWare is ready again to service the queue, at which time it then tries to print again, once more jamming the printer.*

You may have to delete many print jobs from the queue if the user became frustrated and kept trying to resend the same improperly configured print job. Repeatedly sending jobs simply builds up one print job behind another in the queue, to a maximum of 100. Or you may have many print jobs waiting in the queue sent by other users, and as soon as you delete the improperly configured job marked "active" at the head of the queue list, the others will then start to print.

Remember that before you delete the print job, if the user has not saved the original file, copy the print job from the queue subdirectory it is located in to the user's home directory so they do not lose the information.

Core Printing

Core printing services are created automatically in 2.1X NetWare during the operating system installation process and can be chosen during the 2.2 NetWare installation process and then installed and configured at the file server console. During this process, you can assign up to five printers, numbered 0 through 4: three parallel printers to LPT ports and two serial printers to COM ports. NetWare then automatically assigns queues named PRINTQ_0 through PRINTQ_4 to each of those printers and spools devices 0 through 4 to each of those queues.

If you decide later that you wish to add more queues to the printers you defined during the operating system installation process, you can use PCONSOLE to create the queues and then, at the file server console, type `p # add q` *(queue name)*. However, to make this assignment permanent, you must edit the AUTOEXEC.SYS file by using SYSCON. Type **syscon**. Select Supervisor Options, Edit System AUTOEXEC File. Be aware that once you create an AUTOEXEC.SYS file, you must include the default printer, queue, and spool assignments NetWare created during the operating system installation process, or those assignments will be lost. In other words, once you create an AUTOEXEC.SYS file, only the printing information in that file will be utilized by the network. For example, if your default assignment was one printer assigned the printer number 0, the queue printq_0, and the spool number 0, you must include two lines in your AUTOEXEC.SYS file: one that says P 0 ADD PRINTQ_0 to allow you to print to printer 0 through printq_0, and a second line that says S 0 PRINTQ_0 in order to create a spooled device for the queue printq_0.

When this setup is complete, down the file server and reboot it. Core printing services at the file server will now be in effect and you should be able to redirect printing to the file server network printers by using the CAPTURE and NPRINT commands or from inside application programs that have the ability to spool jobs to network devices or queues.

You can check to see if your setup is correct and functional by typing **pconsole** at the workstation. Select Print Queue Information, (*queue name*), and Current Queue Status to see if the queue is attached to a print server. You can also type the commands PRINTER, QUEUE, and SPOOL at the file server console to see a listing of your printers, queues, and spoolers along with their status.

Symptom

You attempt to type a printing command at the file server console and receive the error message "All print and queue commands are now accessed via the print server."

Probable Cause

You are working on a NetWare 2.2 server on which core printing services are not installed and you have tried to use a printing console command.

Solution

On a 2.2 file server, you must use PCONSOLE to execute print server commands. The alternative is to regenerate the operating system using the INSTALL -M command and install core printing.

Symptom

The user receives the error message "Queue does not exist on server," "Invalid printer number specified," "Printer number does not exist on server," or "Printer number is not installed on server" when the user uses the CAPTURE or NPRINT command to direct print jobs to queues or printers.

Probable Cause

The user mistyped the name of the queue or the number of the printer, the queue or the printer does not exist, or the queue or printer was not assigned or was incorrectly assigned in the AUTOEXEC.SYS file.

Solution

Make sure the user has typed the name of the queue and the number of the printer correctly. Use PCONSOLE to check the name of the queue. Type pconsole. Choose Print Queue Information. Or type queue at the file server console. Check printer numbers by typing printer at the file server console. Use SYSCON to check the AUTOEXEC.SYS file. Type syscon. Choose Supervisor Options, Edit System AUTOEXEC File.

Symptom

The printer runs out of paper or the paper jams before the print job is completed. Printing stops and the printer reports an "Out of paper" or "Printer off-line" error message.

Probable Cause

Obviously, the paper holder with tractor-feed paper, the sheet feeder on a dot-matrix printer, or the paper tray on a laserjet printer has run out of paper. Or the tractor feed, sheet feeder, or laserjet paper-feed mechanism has jammed.

Solution

Type p # stop at the file server console, where # is the number of the printer you wish to service. Clear the jam in the printer or add more paper. Type p # mark on a dot-matrix printer to align the top of the form. Type p # start to begin printing again where you left off.

Further Help

From the file server console, you can perform a great many printer control functions with core printing installed—everything from starting and stopping printers to deleting queues and print jobs. See the NetWare 2.1X "Console Commands" manual and the 2.2 "Using the Network" manual for more information.

Print Server

With the addition of the PRINT SERVER VAP and PSERVER.EXE utilities, the function and importance of PCONSOLE for managing the printers and queues on a network have been greatly expanded. PCONSOLE itself has been rewritten to permit the assignment and configuration of multiple print servers and remote printers in addition to queues. PCONSOLE is consequently the main management tool for all printing setup and configuration on the network.

In fact, you must use PCONSOLE before you load the PSERVER VAP at the file server or PSERVER.EXE at a dedicated workstation in order to configure queues, print servers, and printers correctly. Only *after* you have used PCONSOLE for these purposes can you down the file server and reboot it to load the print server and have it work correctly. For a detailed and comprehensive description of installing and using a print server, see the NetWare 2.2 "Print Server" manual.

Symptom

You bring up the file server and are told that "Value Added Processes have been defined," and you are asked if you "wish to load them." You respond by typing y, and you are then asked for the name of the print server. At this point, you either do not know the name or you type it incorrectly. You are then asked for a password. Since there actually is no password, all you can do is press the ENTER key. You are then told there is an error and asked if you wish to abort loading the VAP.

Probable Cause

Either you forgot the name of the print server created with PCONSOLE or you typed it incorrectly.

Solution

Allow the VAP to abort from loading and continue to bring up the file server. Then, from the workstation, log in to the file server and type pconsole. Choose Print Server Information and write down the name of the print server you wish to load. Log out, down the file server, and reboot

it. Type the correct name of the print server when
prompted.

Symptom

You receive the error message "Unable to attach to file
server" while loading the VAP at the file server or running
the PSERVER.EXE command at a dedicated workstation.

Probable Cause

An error prevented the print server from attaching to the
file server or dedicated workstation.

Solution

Down the file server, reboot, and try again. Or at the
workstation, reboot and try again. If the problem persists,
use PCONSOLE to delete all print servers and queues and
reinstall them from scratch. Also, delete the PSERVER.VAP
file from the SYSTEM directory on the file server and copy
it in again from the original NetWare disk. Down and
reboot the file server and try again.

Symptom

You receive the error message "There is already a print
server named (*name of print server*) running" while loading
the VAP at the file server or running the PSERVER.EXE
command at a dedicated workstation.

Probable Cause

Another print server is already running with the name you
have chosen. Every print server must have a unique name.

Solution

Run PCONSOLE and rename the duplicate print server.
Type pconsole. Choose Print Server Information. Highlight

the print server you wish to rename and press the F3 key
on your keyboard. Rename the print server.

Symptom

You attempt to run the PSERVER.EXE command at a
workstation and receive the error message "There are not
enough SPX connections to run the print server."

Probable Cause

The workstation does not have enough SPX connections to
run the PSERVER program.

Solution

Add the line SPX CONNECTIONS = 60 to the SHELL.CFG
file (see Chapter 4, "Workstation Bootup and NetWare Shell
Issues"). Reboot the workstation and run PSERVER.

Symptom

You receive the error message that "The print server does
not exist," or "The print server is not up and running."

Probable Cause

Each of these error messages indicates the cause of the
problem: that is, the named print server does not exist, you
typed the name incorrectly, or the print server is down.

Solution

Use PCONSOLE to make sure the print server name is
spelled correctly and that it exists and to make sure the
print server is up and running. Type pconsole. Choose
Print Server Information, (*print server name*), Print Server
Status Control, File Servers Being Serviced, and press the
INS key. Attach the print server to the file server. Then, at
the file server console, type pserver (*print server name*)
stop. Wait until you are told the print server is down.

Then, type pserver (*print server name*) start to reload
the print server. At that point, the print server will
recognize any changes you have made through
PCONSOLE. If the print server is running on a dedicated
workstation, first down the print server using PCONSOLE,
then reboot the workstation, log in, and run PSERVER.EXE
again. To make sure the print server is up and running,
type pconsole, choose Print Server Information, (*print
server name*), Print Server Status Control, Server Info.

Symptom

You receive the error message "No response from the print
server or print queue cannot be serviced by printer."

Probable Cause

For an unknown reason, the print server cannot respond at
this time.

Solution

Check the print server monitor for a system message. If the
print server continues to hang, down and reboot the file
server and reload the VAP. If the print server is installed at
a dedicated workstation, reboot the print server
workstation and attempt to reload the PSERVER.EXE
program. Type pserver (*name of the print server*) at the
workstation prompt after you log in to the file server.

Symptom

You receive the error message "Insufficient memory to
initialize communications" when you try to load
PSERVER.VAP at the file server or PSERVER.EXE at a
workstation.

Probable Cause

The file server or workstation running PSERVER does not
have enough memory.

Solution

Add memory to the file server. At the workstation, do not load any TSRs.

Symptom

You receive the error message "Not authorized to service queue. Queue will not be serviced by printer" when you try to assign a queue to a printer.

Probable Cause

The print server is not authorized to service the specified queue.

Solution

Type pconsole. Select Print Queue Information, (*print queue name*), Queue Servers, and press the INS key to add the print server to the list of authorized print servers for that queue. Then, at the file server console, type pserver (*print server name*) stop. Wait until you are told the print server is down. Then, type pserver (*print server name*) start to reload the print server or reload PSERVER.EXE at the workstation. At that point, the print server will recognize any changes you have made through PCONSOLE.

Symptom

You receive the error message "Not enough memory: for buffer for printer," "for communications with remote printers," "to add queue to printer," "to add user to notify list for printer," or "to initialize printer number."

Probable Cause

The file server or workstation that is running PSERVER does not have enough memory to perform these operations.

Solution

Add more memory to the file server or workstation.

Symptom

You receive the error message "Unable to get object ID of print server" when you try to load the print server at the file server or workstation running PSERVER.

Probable Cause

The bindery, which must be open to get object IDs, is locked or corrupted.

Solution

Try again in a few minutes. If problems persist, run BINDFIX (see Chapter 3, "The File Server").

Symptom

The user receives the error message "Unable to read configuration file for printer. Printer not initialized" when the user attempts to print to a printer.

Probable Cause

The configuration file for the specified printer is corrupted.

Solution

Type pconsole. Choose Print Server Information, (*print server name*), Print Server Configuration, Printer Configuration. Delete the printer from the print server, and then re-create the printer. Make sure you stop and re-start the print server to make this change take effect.

Symptom

You receive the error message "Illegal print server account name. Unable to attach to file server" when you try to load

the PSERVER.VAP at the file server or PSERVER.EXE at a
dedicated workstation.

Probable Cause

The print server name you are using is not a valid bindery
name—you have mistyped the name, or the name does not
exist.

Solution

Type pconsole. Choose Print Server Information for a list
of defined print servers.

Symptom

You receive the error message "You must be a user or
operator on the print server to issue this command" when
you try to manage the print server.

Probable Cause

You are not defined as a user or operator of the print server
and are not attached to the file server that authorizes you
to view printer status or manage the print server.

Solution

Authorize yourself to be a print server user or operator and
make sure you are attached to that file server. Type
pconsole. Choose Print Server Information, (*print server
name*), Print Server Users, or Print Server Operators, and
press the INS key to make yourself a user or operator.

Remote Printing

Remote printing is available only if you are using the
PSERVER.VAP at the file server or PSERVER.EXE at a

dedicated workstation and have set up a print server with printers identified as remote printers (again, see the NetWare 2.2 "Print Server" manual for details). Once you have established remote printers, any workstation on the network may be assigned as a remote printing workstation so that any other network user can print to the printer attached to that workstation.

The command for installing remote printing on a workstation is RPRINTER. This command brings up a menu screen that identifies the available print servers and then the available remote printers by name and number. If you highlight a printer and press the ENTER key, you will see the message "Remote printer (*name*) installed," and your local printer will now be available to have queues assigned to it for use by other users. You may install more than one remote printer at the workstation, and you may issue the RPRINTER command from a batch file to automate the process. RPRINTER becomes a TSR that takes up approximately 8K of RAM at the workstation each time you load it.

Symptom

The user receives the error message "The printer is not connected or is already in use" or "Unable to select printer on the print server" when the user tries to run RPRINTER.

Probable Cause

An error prevented RPRINTER from selecting the specified printer on the specified print server.

Solution

If the workstation is loading RPRINTER from a batch file that executes every time the workstation boots and this error occurs, the workstation is trying to reconnect before SPX has timed out and removed the printer from the print server's table. Edit the batch file to place a line just above the line that loads RPRINTER that says

RPRINTER (*print server name*) (*printer number*) -R.

This unloads the remote printer from the print server's table before the workstation tries to reload it. If you are not running RPRINTER from a batch file, type `pconsole`. Choose Print Server Information, (*print server name*), Print Server Configuration, Printer Configuration, and make sure the printer number being used is valid and configured properly.

Symptom

The user attempts to run RPRINTER and receives the error message "Unable to get the internetwork address for the indicated print server at this time."

Probable Cause

The bindery is locked and RPRINTER cannot access the bindery information.

Solution

Run BINDFIX if the problem persists for longer than a few minutes (see Chapter 3, "The File Server").

Symptom

The user receives the error message "Insufficient memory" when the workstation tries to load RPRINTER.

Probable Cause

A workstation needs to have 128K of available memory during the initialization of RPRINTER. After it is initialized, it takes only 8K to run.

Solution

Change the order in which programs load at the workstation. Load RPRINTER before you load any applications or TSRs.

Symptom

The user receives the error message "Invalid or wrong number of parameters" when the workstation tries to load RPRINTER.

Probable Cause

The user incorrectly entered the print server name, the printer number, or the -R (remove) parameter.

Solution

Have the user check your typing. Make sure the user separates parameters with spaces.

Symptom

The user receives the error message "No print servers are operating," "The connection with the print server has been lost," "The selected print server could not be found," or "The selected print server does not respond" when the workstation loads RPRINTER.

Probable Cause

No print servers are currently running or the user did not spell the name of the print server correctly when the workstation tried to connect by using RPRINTER. This also occurs if the selected server is hung or if there is some type of connection problem.

Solution

Type pconsole. Choose Print Server Information, (*print server name*), Print Server Status/Control, Server Info to make sure the print server is running.

Symptom

The user receives the error message "Unable to attach to print server" when the workstation runs RPRINTER.

Probable Cause

There are not enough IPX socket connections or SPX connections available at the workstation to attach to the print server.

Solution

Edit the workstation boot disk SHELL.CFG file so it has the correct configurations (see Chapter 4, "Workstation Bootup and NetWare Shell Issues"). The default settings are IPX SOCKETS = 20 and SPX CONNECTIONS = 50. These values may be increased by 10 depending on what other applications are loading in RAM at the workstation.

Symptom

The user receives the error message "All SPX connections in this machine are in use. This application cannot run, until an active connection has terminated or more SPX connections are allocated; or no more IPX sockets are available" when the workstation tries to load RPRINTER.

Probable Cause

Other applications loaded in the workstation are using all defined SPX connections or IPX sockets.

Solution

Increase the SPX CONNECTIONS and IPX SOCKETS parameters in the SHELL.CFG file by at least 10 (the default is 20) and reboot the workstation (see Chapter 4, "Workstation Bootup and NetWare Shell Issues").

Symptom

The user receives the error message "The selected remote printer is already in use" when the workstation tries to run RPRINTER.

Probable Cause

The remote printer selected from the command line is already being used by another workstation.

Solution

Have the user select another remote printer number if one is available. If not, ask the user to wait until the remote printer being used is released by the other workstation.

Special Commands

There are two other special command-line utilities that deserve mention: ENDCAP and PSC. ENDCAP is used to cancel the CAPTURE command and return printing to local printers. PSC is used from a workstation prompt command line to control print server configuration.

Symptom

The user cannot print to their local printer. The job goes to a network printer instead.

Probable Cause

The user did not run ENDCAP or ENDCAP ALL to stop all capturing to network printers and return printing to the local printer at the workstation.

Solution

Have the user type endcap all at the workstation prompt. This ends all resident capture commands and returns printing to the local workstation printer.

➤ *Tech tip:* *This command will, however, have no effect if the application program has been set up internally to direct print jobs to spooled network printers. You may have to access the print control commands in the application program and redirect printing to the local workstation printer ports.*

Symptom

You receive the error message "Invalid printer number specified in DOS environment" when you run PSC from a DOS SET command.

Probable Cause

The printer number specified in the SET PSC command is not a valid printer number.

Solution

Type pconsole. Choose Print Server Information, (*print server name*), Print Server Configuration, Printer Configuration to determine the correct printer number.

Symptom

You receive the error message "You must specify the print server name" when you run PSC from a DOS SET command.

Probable Cause

You did not specify the print server name.

Solution

Specify the print server name or set the default print server with the SET PSC command.

Symptom

You receive the error message "Cannot connect to the print server" when you run the PSC command.

Probable Cause

The print server did not respond to the request from the PSC command.

Solution

Make sure you have typed the correct print server name. If the problem persists, reboot the print server or reload the PSERVER.VAP at the file server.

3

The File Server

The file server is the heart of the network, and when it develops problems, the network has the equivalent of a heart attack. Whether this attack is mild or severe, and whether it calls for symptomatic treatment or major surgery, depends on many factors. The principal factors to consider are the severity of the error messages and how many users are affected.

Not all file server error messages indicate a fatal file server error or halt the operation of the file server. In fact, some messages are not error messages at all but simply status messages to inform you of current operating system conditions. Other error messages simply indicate the file server has experienced a problem but the operating system will automatically fix the problem without your intervention. However, there are those error messages that indicate a very severe problem has occurred and you must intervene.

Sometimes the problem affects only a few users, usually those who are working with the same application program or database. Sometimes the problem is network wide and all users are affected, regardless of the application program being used. Sometimes the file server operating system is still working. Sometimes the operating system is completely shut down.

In all cases, problems that affect the file server are the most cause for concern of any network problems. The file server is, after all, the storage area for precious records and files, and the engine servicing distributed processing. The network simply does not exist unless the file server is running correctly.

Before proceeding to the topic of common operating system problems, it is important to point out that, unlike other chapters, the solutions in this chapter refer you often to the NetWare manuals. This is necessary because solving operating system problems often involves a regeneration and/or reinstallation of the operating system at the file server. It is far beyond the scope of this book to provide the detailed instructions for performing those operations.

However, you need to be aware, especially if you are relatively new to NetWare, that you should have at hand or at least always know the whereabouts of the specially configured disk copies of the original red-labeled NetWare disks shipped in the NOVELL box. These disk copies were used by the installer to configure NetWare for your file server hardware. These disk copies are normally created during the 2.1*X* installation process when, before exiting from ELSGEN (ELS NetWare) or NETGEN (Advanced or SFT NetWare), you are asked if you wish to download files to floppy disk. If you answer yes, ELSGEN or NETGEN prompts you for the disk copies you have made of the ELSGEN or NETGEN disks named SUPPORT, OSEXE-1, OSEXE-2, UTILEXE-1 (ELS is UTIL-1), and UTILEXE-2 (ELS is UTIL-2). It then loads onto those disks the operating system you have just linked and configured. In NetWare 2.2, you must type download at the DOS prompt after you exit from INSTALL in order to accomplish the same thing. You are then prompted for the disk copies you have made of the SYSTEM-1, SYSTEM-2, and OSEXE disks.

If you do not have these configured disks, you cannot make any maintenance changes to the operating system, reinstall the operating system, or run hard disk utilities such as VREPAIR or DISKED without first regenerating the operating system again from scratch. Unfortunately, all too frequently NetWare dealers and consultants install NetWare at a client's site and do not leave a copy of these critical disks on site. In the worst case, they may not even have

made or kept a copy themselves. If you do not have these
disks (and remember, they are disk copies of the original
red-labeled NetWare disks, and they are uniquely
configured for your system—you *cannot* use the original
red-labeled NetWare disks for this purpose), you must
either get them from the original installer if possible or
generate them yourself. If you have little or no experience
with NetWare and the ins and outs of uploading and
configuring special LAN drivers or disk drivers, you should
contact an authorized NOVELL dealer for assistance before
you attempt this process. And, of course, before you
attempt any maintenance, reinstallation, or utility service
procedure at the file server, always make sure you have a
complete, up-to-date, and verified backup on hand!

Routing and Configuration

Routing and configuration errors are often caused by
setting critical parameters at the file server too low or by
too much demand on available file server resources. These
conditions may reflect an error on the part of the installer
who did not properly configure the network, or they may
be the result of problems that develop over time as the
network grows, more workstations are added, traffic grows
over the network, and demands on the file server increase.

The response to these errors is generally determined by the
nature of the error message being generated. However, the
response usually falls into one of several broad categories:
reduce the load on the LAN by dividing the network into
several LANs through the installation of internal or external
bridges or routers, increase the amount of file server
memory available for critical core functions such as file
service processes in the dynamic memory pool area, install
more memory at the file server to increase file caching,

adjust functional parameters such as the number of communication buffers or the number of maximum files open to adequately meet expected demand, and increase the amount of hard disk space available.

Any of these responses involves, to a greater or lesser degree, reconfiguring and reinstalling the operating system. For NetWare 2.1*X*, this means you must carefully read and follow the directions in the NetWare "Installation" and "Maintenance" manuals and for NetWare 2.2, the directions in the "Installing and Maintaining the Network" manual. Pay particular attention to the instructions for reconfiguring and relinking LAN drivers and disk drivers and for performing a "Custom" and "Miscellaneous Maintenance" (2.1*X*) or INSTALL -M -L (2.2) installation at the file server. Remember that COMPSURF stands for "comprehensive surface analysis" and involves an extensive read/write test of the hard drive surface and the ability of the hard drive's read/write head positioning mechanism to perform rapid "seeks." Any COMPSURF test of the drive is therefore completely destructive of all information on the drive.

Also remember the general rules for maintenance service on the file server. If you add or change LAN drivers or disk drivers, you must perform a two-step process. You must first regenerate the operating system, usually at a computer other than the file server. Second, you must then reinstall the operating system at the file server. If you are making performance adjustments only to the existing server configuration, you need not regenerate the operating system as long as the installation disks used to install the operating system on the file server originally are available. You can use these disks to adjust the system for better performance. Finally, a file server can have as many as four LAN cards installed in it, running on four separate cabling systems. In addition, external bridges (now called routers in NetWare 2.2) can be set up in dedicated or nondedicated workstations to expand the network and to divide network traffic over several more LANs.

Before you perform either a reinstallation or performance adjustment of the file server, always make sure you have a complete, verified backup of the file server, all users are logged out of the file server, and you have properly brought the file server down by typing the command DOWN at the file server console before you proceed. Boot the server back up with a DOS disk in drive A. Reload the operating system by placing the ELSGEN (2.1*X* ELS NetWare) or NETGEN (2.1*X* Advanced and SFT NetWare) disk in drive A and typing the command ELSGEN -C OR NETGEN -C (-C for Custom) in NetWare 2.1*X*, and by placing the SYSTEM-1 disk in drive A and typing the command INSTALL -M -L (for Maintenance Link) in NetWare 2.2.

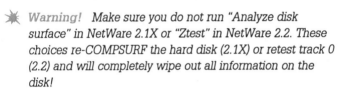

Warning!   Make sure you do not run "Analyze disk surface" in NetWare 2.1X or "Ztest" in NetWare 2.2. These choices re-COMPSURF the hard disk (2.1X) or retest track 0 (2.2) and will completely wipe out all information on the disk!

Also note that you can make some of the required performance changes by using the command DCONFIG, thereby completely avoiding reloading the operating system at the file server.

Symptom

At the file server console, you receive the error message "ERROR! Address collision with (*servername*)" or "ROUTER CONFIGURATION ERROR!!! Router # claims LAN A is #!"

Probable Cause

At least two networks have been set up, and they are both using the same network address. You cannot have two LANs on an internetwork with the same network address.

Only file servers, external bridges, or routers on the *same* LAN can have the same network address.

Solution

Change the network address of one of the file server LANs or the address of one of the LANs in the external router so it is different from all other LAN addresses. You can use NETGEN -C in NetWare 2.1*X* or INSTALL -M in NetWare 2.2 to make this change at the file server. However, it is much easier and faster to use the DCONFIG.EXE program shipped with NetWare to change the network address of a LAN card in the file server: make sure all users are logged out, and log in to the file server as supervisor. Then, type cd\system. Next, type flag net$os.exe n to change the operating system file to Normal (Non-Shareable Read/Write). Copy DCONFIG.EXE from the NetWare 2.1*X* SHGEN-1 disk or the NetWare 2.2 WSGEN disk into the SYSTEM directory. Then, type dconfig net$os.exe (*a, b, c, or d*): #, where the letter is the LAN you wish to change and # is the new, unique network address you wish to assign to that LAN. This can be any eight-digit HEX number except all zeros or all F's. Finally, type flag net$ os.exe sro to return NET$OS.EXE to a Shareable Read Only condition. Log out, down the file server, and reboot it.

For an external bridge or router, you will have to regenerate the BRIDGE.EXE or ROUTER.EXE file that you use to bring up the bridge or router. See your NetWare 2.1*X* "Maintenance" manual or your NetWare 2.2 "Installing and Maintaining the Network" manual for the steps for performing this procedure.

Symptom

Network performance degrades, there are longer waits for information to be sent to the server, or connections to the server are repeatedly lost.

Probable Cause

Workstation hardware or cabling may be the cause of this problem (see Chapter 5, "Workstation Hardware" and Chapter 6, "Cabling"), or the number of file service processes (FSPs) is so low that the workstation cannot be serviced. This problem also appears on ARCnet when two workstation nodes have the same address.

Solution

If the error message is the result of a low number of file service processes, you will have to increase the number of FSPs available at the file server. The very best way to do this under NetWare 2.1X is to decrease the size of the packet used by the LAN cards. You will have to regenerate the operating system and reinstall it at the file server. You may also try lowering the number of configured printers and reducing the number of drive mappings, but these changes usually do not release enough memory in dynamic memory pool 1 (DMP 1) to affect the number of available FSPs. In NetWare 2.2, this problem has been greatly reduced, if not eliminated, because drive mappings have been taken completely out of DMP 1 and placed in a new DMP 4 location, thus freeing more memory for FSPs.

➤ *Tech tip:* *A file service process is analogous to a bellboy at a hotel. As packages arrive at the hotel front desk, the bell captain rings for a bellboy to deliver the package to the correct room. The fewer the number of bellboys available, the more packages stack up at the front desk waiting for delivery. In a file service process, as packets are received for delivery at the file server, the operating system attempts to deliver them to the correct location in the file server. It makes use of FSPs for this delivery, and the fewer they are in number, the slower the delivery occurs and the more packets are routed into a waiting line for delivery.*

NetWare provides a maximum of ten FSPs to start. The recommended minimum is three or four. You can check to see if you have an adequate number of FSPs by using FCONSOLE at a workstation. Log in as supervisor and type fconsole. Choose Statistics, LAN I/O Statistics. Divide the number in the File Service Used Route (the delivery waiting line) by the Total Packets Received. The result should be under ten percent.

Further Help

See the *NetWare Server Troubleshooting and Maintenance Handbook*, by Edward Liebing and Ken Neff (LAN TIMES/McGraw-Hill, 1990) for a full discussion of the FSP problem.

Symptom

The user receives a "Disk I/O read error" at the workstation when he or she attempts to read a file from the file server.

Probable Cause

The file server is too busy processing other network requests or there is a problem with an internal hardware component such as a disk drive, a controller, or RAM.

Solution

Have the user wait a few minutes and try the command again. If the error persists, type fconsole at the workstation. Choose Statistics, Summary. Or type config at the file server console. Either command will allow you to determine the number of file service processes available. If the number is below two, this may be the problem, in which case you need to increase the number of FSPs by regenerating the operating system and lowering the packet size of your LAN driver or, if this is not possible, upgrade to NetWare 2.2.

If the number of FSPs is adequate (usually at least three), you may have a disk drive or controller problem in the file server. First try replacing the hard drive controller cables. If the problem persists, replace the controller with an identical new controller. If the problem continues, you will have to back up all data and either re-COMPSURF or replace the hard drive in the file server (see the section entitled "File Server Bootup" later in this chapter). Finally, if you are having trouble with only one file, copying the file and then erasing the old copy might solve the problem.

Symptom

The user receives the error message "File server has no free connection slots" when he or she attempts to log in or attach to a file server.

Probable Cause

The user is trying to log in more workstations than the version of NetWare permits. Keep in mind that even though NetWare 2.1X ELS I, ELS II, Advanced, and SFT are sold as 4-, 8-, and 100-user versions respectively, when you add a value added process (VAP), a value added disk driver (VADD), or a nondedicated file server DOS process, you use up logical connection slots at the server. This error message may also be caused by workstation hardware or cable failure (see Chapter 5, "Workstation Hardware" and Chapter 6, "Cabling").

Solution

Have the user wait a few minutes and try again. If the error continues on a regular basis, you may have to upgrade to NetWare 2.2, which provides additional connection slots for these extra processes above the actual number reserved for users. For example, the 50-user version of NetWare 2.2 actually provides 66 logical connections to the file server, 50 for users, and 16 for other processes that require a logical connection. If you have not exceeded the number of available connection slots, proceed to diagnose the problem as a workstation hardware or cabling problem (see Chapter 5, "Workstation Hardware" and Chapter 6, "Cabling").

Symptom

The file server returns the error message "Invalid number of FCBs requested from configuration information" as it starts to boot up.

Probable Cause

The maximum number of files that can be open simultaneously is set to fewer than 20 or greater than 1000. Track 0 information has been corrupted, or the cable, controller, hard drive, or memory has failed.

Solution

Use ELSGEN or NETGEN -C (NetWare 2.1X) or INSTALL -F (NetWare 2.2) to change the number of open files to between 20 and 1000. Then reboot the file server. If the error continues, reinstall the entire operating system. If the error persists, check and replace memory- or disk-related hardware.

Symptom

Performance degrades at the file server so that application programs take a long time to retrieve files from the server. This may result in "Network error on server" error messages that clear after several retries. You may also get file server error messages such as "No free space to verify FAT tables," "Not enough memory for disk FAT tables," "Not enough memory to cache volume," or "Not enough memory available for cache blocks."

Probable Cause

There is not enough RAM available at the file server to adequately cache files. Therefore, the operating system is "thrashing" cache blocks and the number of reads from the cache, as opposed to reads from the physical disk, is very low.

Solution

Log in as supervisor from the workstation and run FCONSOLE. Type fconsole. Choose Statistics, CACHE Statistics. The thrashing count should be very low and the number of cache reads compared to physical disk reads should be very high. Press the ESC key to close this window, and go to Summary. The percent of cache reads from disk should be over 80 percent and preferably 95 percent or greater. This is especially true if you are using large database programs. If the percentage is less than 80 percent, add more RAM to the server.

➤ *Tech tip: NetWare will automatically use the extra RAM at the file server for file caching as soon as it is installed. You need only reboot the file server. The minimum amount of RAM for a 2.1X file server is 2 megabytes, and for a 2.2 file server it is 2 1/2 megabytes. However, given the large size of hard disks today and the number of increased services, 4 megabytes of RAM is a safer base number to use.*

Symptom

The user receives a "Not enough file handles open" error message at the workstation when he or she attempts to run a network application program.

Probable Cause

You do not have enough files open on the file server for all of the application program demands.

Solution

Log in as supervisor and run FCONSOLE to check the number of files open at the server. Type fconsole. Choose Statistics, Summary. Look at the maximum number of files open compared to the peak used. If this number is close, log out, down the file server, and use ELSGEN or NETGEN -C (NetWare 2.1X) or INSTALL -F (NetWare 2.2) to increase the number of open files.

Symptom

The user receives a "File server cannot be found" error message at the workstation, but all other workstations are attached. You check for workstation and cabling problems, but none can be found (see Chapter 4, "Workstation Bootup and NetWare Shell Issues," Chapter 5, "Workstation Hardware," and Chapter 6, "Cabling").

Probable Cause

The file server has run out of communication buffers. The rule of thumb is that you need ten communication buffers for every LAN card in the file server and two communication buffers for every workstation.

Solution

Go to another workstation, log in as supervisor, and run FCONSOLE. Type fconsole. Choose Statistics, Summary. Look at the Maximum setting for communication buffers compared to the peak used. If all are used, no workstations can attach to the file server until some are freed up. You can log out all users, down the file server, and use ELSGEN or NETGEN -C (NetWare 2.1X) or INSTALL -M (NetWare 2.2) to increase the number of communication buffers. Or you can use DCONFIG. Make sure all users are logged out, and log in to the file server as supervisor. Then, type cd\system Next, type flag net$os.exe n to change the operating system file to Normal (Non-Shareable Read/Write). Copy DCONFIG.EXE from the NetWare 2.1X SHGEN-1 disk or the NetWare 2.2 WSGEN disk into the SYSTEM directory. Then, type dconfig net$os.exe buffers:#, where # is the higher number of communication buffers you wish to assign to that LAN, up to 250 in NetWare 2.1X and 1000 in NetWare 2.2. Finally, type flag net$os.exe sro to return NET$OS.EXE to a Shareable Read Only condition. Log out, down the file server, and reboot it.

Symptom

The user receives the error message "Out of directory entries" at the workstation. The user cannot create files or directories on the file server.

Probable Cause

The user is storing large numbers of small files on the file server, each of which uses up one directory entry. There may be plenty of room left on the file server hard disk that cannot be used because the total number of directory entries on the file server is exhausted.

Solution

Log in as supervisor and type chkvol. If the number of available directory entries is 0, the simplest solution is to delete all unnecessary files from the volume to free up directory entries. If you cannot delete a sufficient number of files, run ELSGEN or NETGEN -C for NetWare 2.1X or INSTALL -F for NetWare 2.2 and increase the number of directory entries available on the volume. The maximum number available depends on the size of the volume, up to a maximum of 10,000.

Symptom

You attempt to log in to the file server as supervisor and get an "Access denied" error message even though you have typed the password correctly. You may not even be able to log in as a user.

Probable Cause

The supervisor password has been changed or lost, or the bindery is corrupt.

Solution

Use the NetWare DISKED.EXE program to edit the sector location on the file server where the bindery files NET$BIND.SYS and NET$BVAL.SYS are stored. The task here is to change the extension on these files to something other than SYS. The easiest change is to make the files end in SSS. When you reboot the file server, NetWare will ignore these renamed bindery files and assume no bindery exists, as if you were booting up the file server for the first time. NetWare will then create a new set of bindery files and you will be able to log in as supervisor with no password, just as you would log in to a newly installed file server.

✳ *Warning!* *DISKED is a dangerous program to use if you are not very familiar with NetWare.*

DISKED.EXE can be found on the NetWare 2.1X UTILEXE-2 disk. However, it is no longer linked and configured in NetWare 2.2 during the operating system generation process. The reason is that the program allows anyone with access to the server to bring the file server down, reboot with DOS and, if there is no power-on or keyboard password, run DISKED and bypass network security. NOVELL therefore removed it from NetWare 2.2. However, if you have a standard ST506/412 or ESDI disk drive, any DISKED program linked and configured in NetWare 2.1X for that type of drive will work on a NetWare 2.2 server.

If you must use DISKED, you need to understand hexadecimal and how to perform a sector edit on a NetWare hard disk. Use caution! You must be extremely careful not to write incorrect information to the file server hard disk and not to write the changes you make to the wrong sector. You could lose all access to the file server. Unless you are experienced with NetWare and the sector editing process, you should contact a NOVELL authorized dealer or reseller for assistance using DISKED.

File Server Bootup

If the file server boots up correctly, you will see messages indicating the "cold boot loader" and operating system are loading correctly, the volumes are mounting, and the LAN drivers are being installed. You will then see a message about the version of NetWare you are using, and you will end up at a colon (:) prompt. If you then type the word monitor, you will see six station activity boxes on the file server monitor.

The file server may fail to boot properly for a number of reasons. The most common failures have to do with power supply failures; insufficient RAM or RAM failure; hard drive track 0 or hard drive controller failure; LAN card failure or configuration conflict; corruption of the operating system file NET$OS.EXE; corruption of the partition, volume, or file allocation table information on the hard disk; or corruption of the bindery files NET$BIND.SYS and NET$BVAL.SYS, which store information about users, groups, rights, and so forth.

Symptom

The error message "!!!VOLUME MOUNT ERROR — NO FREE ALLOCATION SPACE!!!" appears on the file server console during bootup.

Probable Cause

Dynamic memory pool 1 has run out of memory.

Solution

Decrease the demands on this memory pool by running ELSGEN or NETGEN -C in NetWare 2.1X and eliminating unused printer configurations at the file server. Try to log in again and then reduce the number of drive mappings being used on the network by editing the system and user login scripts (see Chapter 1, "System Management"). You can also upgrade to NetWare 2.2, which has eliminated many dynamic memory pool demand problems.

Symptom

At the file server you receive the error message "Not enough memory for security tables," or to "Add the VAP," "Hash directories," or "Cache a volume." The file server shuts down or does not load the VAP.

Probable Cause

RAM failed in the server or you need to add more RAM.

Solution

Use a RAM test program like CheckIt to test RAM at the file server, or add more RAM. NetWare 2.X can use up to 12 megabytes of RAM in the file server, with a minimum of 2 megabytes for NetWare 2.1X and 2 1/2 megabytes for

NetWare 2.2. However, VAPs, larger hard drives, and more workstation demand all require more RAM at the server. Four megabytes is the suggested minimum for most installations today.

Symptom

At the file server you receive the error message "Attempt to configure a non-operating drive. Repair or remove drive from the system."

Probable Cause

The hard drive, hard drive cable, or controller has failed.

Solution

Make sure all cables are secure and all connections are tight. Remove the hard drive controller from its slot in the system board and clean the gold finger connections with a pencil eraser or cleaning solution made for this purpose. Replace the controller and try again. If problems persist, replace the controller with an exact duplicate. If problems still persist, re-COMPSURF or replace the hard disk.

➤ *Tech tip: Obviously, this is the most fatal of all problems and requires a complete reinstallation of the network operating system. Note that this solution depends on the existence of a current backup of all programs and data to avoid excessive down time and data loss.*

Further Help

Your NetWare 2.1X "Installation" and "Maintenance" manuals and your NetWare 2.2 "Installing and Maintaining the Network" manual have complete descriptions for performing a hard drive COMPSURF and for reinstallation of NetWare.

Symptom

At the file server, you receive the error message "Drive not set up for Hot Fix," "Error reading disk redirection data or tables," or "Error reading disk redirection information on sector 14." If the drive is the first drive with volume SYS on it, the file server will not boot up and the error is fatal.

Probable Cause

The Hot Fix area has been lost on the drive, or the cables, controller, or drive itself has failed.

Solution

Run NETGEN -C (NetWare 2.1X) or INSTALL -M -L (NetWare 2.2) to reestablish Hot Fix on the drive. If the error persists, back up all files and repair or replace the hard drive.

Symptom

You receive the error message "Primary drive has failed, switching to mirrored drive" at the file server console.

Probable Cause

The primary hard disk had failed and mirroring has changed to the secondary drive.

Solution

When time is available, shut down the file server and remove the primary drive. Repair or replace it in the file server and remirror the drive. Consult your NetWare 2.1X "Maintenance Manual" or your NetWare 2.2 "Installing and Maintaining the Network" and "Concepts" manuals for details on drive mirroring.

Symptom

At the file server you receive the error message "Error reading the bad block table, or sector 14 or 15, of the new mirrored drive," or "Error reading mirror information on ALL drives at the file server."

Probable Cause

The cable, controller, or mirrored drive itself has failed. Hot Fix has been lost.

Solution

Use NETGEN -C (SFT NetWare 2.1X) or INSTALL -M -L (NetWare 2.2) to reestablish Hot Fix on the drive. If the errors persist, check and replace cables, reseat the controller, or replace the controller or drive.

Symptom

At the file server you receive the error message "Background re-mirror aborted due to drive shut down" or "due to ten write errors in a row," or "Drive was shut down due to an unrecoverable failure and cannot be re-mirrored."

Probable Cause

The controller, cables, or drive you are remirroring has failed. The remirroring process aborts.

Solution

Repair or replace the defective components, and then remirror the drive using NETGEN (SFT NetWare 2.1X) or INSTALL (NetWare 2.2). If you are using a disk controller board (DCB) and an external expansion box for the mirrored drive, make sure it is powered on before you attempt the remirroring process.

Further Help

See the NetWare 2.1*X* "Maintenance" manual and the NetWare 2.2 "Concepts" manual for a discussion of mirroring. Remember that you must have the SFT level II version of NetWare 2.1*X* to establish mirroring. All user levels (5, 10, 50, or 100) of NetWare 2.2 come with mirroring and duplexing features built in.

Symptom

You receive the error message "WARNING! LAN (*letter*) DEAD" or "failed to initialize LAN (*letter*)" as you boot up the file server. The file server automatically shuts itself down.

Probable Cause

The network board for that LAN has either completely failed or has the wrong IRQ, base I/O, or base memory address settings or is the wrong manufacturer's card for the LAN driver software you selected when you generated the operating system.

Solution

In the first instance, open the file server and check the network board for proper seating. Try again. If it fails again, replace the network board. In the second instance, either reset the jumpers and switches on the network board (see Chapter 5, "Workstation Hardware") to match your operating system LAN configuration, or use DCONFIG to change your LAN configuration to match your board settings. Type **cd\system**. Next, type **flag net$os.exe n** to change the operating system file to Normal (Non-Shareable Read/Write). Copy DCONFIG.EXE from the NetWare 2.1*X* SHGEN-1 disk or the NetWare 2.2 WSGEN disk into the SYSTEM directory. Then, type **dconfig net$os.exe (*a, b, c, or d*):#,,#**, where the letter is the LAN you wish to change, the first # is the network address, and the second # is the LAN configuration option number you wish to use. Finally, type **flag net$os.exe sro** to return NET$OS.EXE to a Shareable Read Only condition. Log out, down the file server, and reboot it. In the third instance, if you have a driver selected for the the wrong manufacturer's card, you must regenerate the operating system to match the board settings and manufacturer. Use ELSGEN or NETGEN -C (NetWare 2.1X) or INSTALL -M (NetWare 2.2).

Symptom

You receive the error message "Error, hole in file" when you boot up the file server.

Probable Cause

The NET$OS.EXE operating system file in the SYSTEM directory on volume SYS is corrupted.

Solution

Reboot the file server with a DOS disk in drive A. Find the configured disk copies of the OSEXE-1 and OSEXE-2 disks in NetWare 2.1X or the OSEXE disk in NetWare 2.2. Place the OSEXE-1 disk or the OSEXE disk in drive A and type net$os. (NetWare 2.1X will then prompt you for the OSEXE-2 disk.) If the operating system loads successfully, the file server will come up and you will be able to log in. Once you are sure this works, log out, down the file server, reboot it with DOS, and use ELSGEN or NETGEN -C in NetWare 2.1X or INSTALL -M -L in NetWare 2.2 to reload the operating system onto the file server hard disk.

Symptom

You receive the error message "ERROR—CANNOT OPEN BINDERY FILES at the file server."

Probable Cause

The bindery files, NET$BVAL.SYS and NET$BIND.SYS, have been corrupted or no longer exist on volume SYS in the SYSTEM directory.

Solution

The system will try to create new files so you can log in to the file server as supervisor. If you can log in as supervisor, restore the original bindery files from a backup, then type `cd\system`, and then type `bindfix`. This runs the NetWare BINDFIX.EXE program, which will check the bindery and correct any problems. If the file server fails to create new bindery files, you may not have enough RAM in the server or you may need to increase the number of available directory entries. Use NETGEN C (NetWare 2.1*X*) or INSTALL -M (NetWare 2.2) to increase the number of directory entries. Add more RAM. If you continue to be denied login access to the file server, you can use DISKED to disable the current bindery files. (See the end of the preceding section, "Routing and Configuration," for a discussion of DISKED.)

Symptom

The error message "Invalid .VAP header" appears at the file server.

Probable Cause

A value added process (VAP) is corrupted as it tries to load.

Solution

Reinstall the VAP from original disks. First, log in as supervisor and type `cd\system`. Place the disk with the VAP in drive A and copy the VAP file from drive A into the SYSTEM directory. Log out, down the file server, and reboot. If the problem persists, contact the vendor who supplied the VAP.

Symptom

You receive an "NMI interrupt" or "Parity error" error message at the file server when you boot up. The file server operating system "abends," that is, it comes to an abnormal end, causing a fatal error that shuts down the file server.

Probable Cause

The CPU received a pulse on its Non-Maskable Interrupt line, indicating a problem with RAM.

Solution

First, reboot the file server. NMI and parity errors are often transient and simply rebooting the file server will clear them. They can be merely the result of a corrupted program or operating system file loading into the file server. If the problem persists, use ELSGEN or NETGEN -C in NetWare 2.1X or INSTALL -M -L in NetWare 2.2 to reload the operating system onto the file server hard disk. If the problem continues, run a memory test program such as CheckIt on the file server to identify possible memory conflicts or bad RAM. You may need to change base I/O or base memory addresses on your LAN cards and regenerate the operating system with ELSGEN or NETGEN -C (NetWare 2.1X) or INSTALL -M (NetWare 2.2) to match the new board configurations. (See Chapter 4, "Workstation Bootup and NetWare Shell Issues" and Chapter 5, "Workstation Hardware" for a longer discussion of memory addresses.) If there are no conflicts and the problem continues, run a RAM test program at the file server and replace the indicated bad RAM chips.

Symptom

You receive the error message "*** WARNING *** Directory sector # data mirror mismatch," "FATAL DIR ERROR ON VOL (*name*) DIR SECTOR #," or "FATAL DIR ERROR ON VOL (*name*) FAT SECTOR #" when you boot up the file server. You are asked if you wish to "MOUNT THE VOLUME" or not.

Probable Cause

The file server lost power or was turned off without the DOWN command being issued. As a result, a sector was updated without the mirrored FAT being updated or the mirrored FAT and directory tables in the mirrored FAT and directory could not be read.

Solution

These are serious and potentially harmful error messages that should not be ignored, and they are often accompanied by many other error messages. There are probably significant problems in the directory and FAT areas, and if you proceed to mount the volumes and allow users to write to the hard disk, you risk increasing the problem and possibly losing large amounts of data on the volume. You should answer no to the question of whether or not to mount the volume. Then, reboot the file server using a DOS disk. Place the configured disk copy of the NetWare 2.1X UTILEXE-2 or the NetWare 2.2 SYSTEM-2 disk in drive A and type vrepair. This runs the VREPAIR.EXE program configured for your file server's hard drive and controller. VREPAIR will read the volume and attempt to correct FAT, directory, and data errors on the volume.

➤ *Tech tip: Never run VREPAIR on the same volume twice without rebooting the file server onto the drive A DOS disk between attempts. You can seriously damage volume information if you do. Also, VREPAIR as it is shipped on the original disks by NOVELL will work on most industry standard (ISA) type drives—that is, ST506/412 and ESDI. However, it will not work on drives attached to DCBs, SCSI controllers, or the newer IDE drives. It is always good practice to run only the VREPAIR configured during the operating system generation for your file server.*

Symptom

You receive the error message "** WARNING ** Sector # DIR (or FAT) Table # read error on (*volume*)" when you boot up the file server.

Probable Cause

The operating system could not read a sector from the volume's FAT or directory. The file server lost power or was turned off without the DOWN command being used.

Solution

You can continue to run the file server if necessary; however, it is best to not mount the volume and to use VREPAIR to correct the problem. Until you run VREPAIR, the directory and FAT mirror will not function correctly for this sector.

Symptom

You receive the error message "*** WARNING *** FAT Entry # out of bounds" or "out of order" in (*filename*) when you boot up the file server.

Probable Cause

The file server lost power or was turned off without the DOWN command being issued so FAT file links and physical disk entries are either truncated or out of order.

Solution

This is not a fatal error; however, the file in question is probably corrupted and should be erased and restored from backup. VREPAIR might repair the problem, and if no backup exists, VREPAIR can be tried.

Symptom

The error message "*** WARNING *** FAT entry # marked used with no file" appears when you boot up the file server.

Probable Cause

The file server lost power or was turned off without the DOWN command being issued and after one sector was updated but before its mirror sector was updated. The file server has detected that it has a disk block allocated to a file but no file linked to the disk block.

Solution

Allow the file server volume to mount. The file server automatically deallocates the block and repairs itself. You do not need to run VREPAIR.

File Server Operation

The file server normally performs its day-to-day work out of sight and out of mind. It is often placed in a secure area away from routine traffic. In many installations, it is left running 24 hours a day and only brought down occasionally for a maintenance cleaning. If a NetWare file server is built from quality components, has proper power conditioning, and is kept in a cool and protected environment, it is unusual to have to service it for preventive maintenance more than once or twice a year.

However, as with any machine containing complex moving parts, electronic components, and a powerful operating system rich in features, problems can and do develop during the operational life of the server. These problems usually break down into those having to do with the hard disk, those having to do with memory, and those having to do with the operating system software.

Hard disk problems can develop over time and can be monitored through either FCONSOLE at the workstation or the DISK command at the file server console. The most important statistic to track is the use of the hard disk's Hot Fix area. During the installation process, NetWare sets aside two percent of the hard disk area for Hot Fix purposes (unless you specify more). This area is used by NetWare to redirect any write attempts to bad blocks on the hard disk surface (one block is 4096 bytes). If NetWare attempts to write to the surface of the disk and cannot then perform an immediate read after write verification of the data it has just written, it redirects the write to a block location in the Hot Fix area it sets aside on the innermost tracks of the hard disk. Thus, the more this area is used, the more bad spots are developing on the hard disk surface. The general rule of thumb is that when 80 percent of the Hot Fix area is used up, plans should be made to replace the hard disk.

Memory problems usually develop from overheating, static electricity, or voltage fluctuations. RAM chips can fail temporarily or permanently, and when they do, file server operation comes to an immediate halt.

Operating system problems can result from either hard disk failure or memory problems or can develop from accidental rebooting of the file server without its being properly downed first. When this happens, you may also find the bindery corrupted. The bindery is made up of information stored in two files, NET$BVAL.SYS and NET$BIND.SYS.

These files hold information about user and group bindery objects and are critical to proper continuous functioning of the file server.

Symptom

You receive the file server error message "Channel # was shut down due to unrecoverable failure" or "Configured disk coprocessor is not responding," "got a premature interrupt," "had a memory failure," "had a ROM checksum failure," "returned an error code," "could not be configured," or "timed out."

Probable Cause

A disk channel # shuts down or a disk coprocessor board (DCB) fails because of an interrupt or time-out problem. The problem may be faulty cabling, a bad controller, or a failed hard disk.

Solution

Test to make sure all cables are connected and controllers are properly seated. Clean all controller and DCB connectors, reseat the boards, and try again. Make sure you have installed a terminating resistor on the *first* and *last* controller and the *last* drive connected to the DCB bus. If the error persists, replace, in order, the cables, controller, and hard disk.

➤   *Tech tip: If this problem develops with channel 0, the error is fatal and the file server will shut down. Channel 0 controls the first hard disk with volume SYS installed. The other channels—1, 2, 3, and 4—are attached to either a NOVELL disk coprocessor board or a third-party small computer systems interface (SCSI) hard drive controller. If these channels fail, you will lose access to the information on the hard drives attached to them, but the network will continue to operate. Note that the term "host bus adapter" (HBA) is now often used to describe a DCB or SCSI controller.*

Symptom

The error message "Transaction tracking disabled due to running out of disk space" appears at the file server.

Probable Cause

There is less than 1 megabyte of space left on your hard disk in volume SYS. This is the minimum amount of free disk space required by NetWare's transaction tracking system (TTS).

Solution

Delete unneeded files on volume SYS. Then type enable transactions at the file server console.

➤ *Tech tip: You must be using 2.1X SFT level II NetWare or NetWare 2.2 to have transaction tracking available (see Chapter 5, "Workstation Hardware," for a description of how NetWare TTS works).*

Symptom

You receive the error message "General protection interrupt" or "Invalid drive passed to disk process" at the file server and the server shuts down with an abend (abnormal end).

Probable Cause

The CPU's registers or the file server's memory has been severely altered, usually because of a memory failure caused by power fluctuations or a corrupted operating system.

Solution

Reboot the file server. If the error persists, reinstall the operating system using ELSGEN or NETGEN -C (NetWare 2.1*X*) or INSTALL -M -L (NetWare 2.2). If the problem continues to occur, check power conditioning, file server RAM, the hard disk controller, or the hard drive.

Symptom

You receive the error message "Write Error: dir = # file = (*filename*) vol = (*volume name*)" at the file server.

Probable Cause

The operating system could not complete the read-after-write verification of a hard disk write. This error message never occurs if Hot Fix is active unless the file is seriously corrupted. This error message usually indicates that a location on the hard disk has gone bad to the extent that it cannot retain data or the electronics on the hard disk controller, DCB, or hard disk itself are faulty.

Solution

Use VREPAIR to try to fix the problem (see the earlier section, "File Server Bootup"). If the problem persists, replace the hard disk cables, controllers, and hard disk, in that order.

Symptom

You receive the error message "Hot fix has been turned off on drive # volume (*name*)" at the file server. You begin to experience "Errors writing to file" error messages at workstations and at the file server.

Probable Cause

The disk redirection area is full or Hot Fix could not write and verify data ten times in a row. This indicates severe problems with the hard drive. It is also possible NetWare was improperly installed and the hard drive was low-level formatted with more than 1024 cylinders. Since DOS cannot work properly on hard drives larger than 1024 cylinders, Hot Fix redirection fails.

Solution

Type `disk` at the file server console to check the status of Hot Fix. If there is no room left, the drive will need to be completely backed up, COMPSURF (2.1X NetWare) or ZTEST (2.2 NetWare) run at the file server, and the operating system reinstalled to increase the size of Hot Fix. However, in this situation, the drive is probably failing to the extent that you are better off replacing it. If you can, type `fconsole`. Choose Statistics, Disk Statistics and see how many cylinders and heads are identified for the drive. If you are using Netware 2.1x, and the drive has more than 1024 cylinders, it may indicate the drive was simply not installed properly and there is nothing physically wrong with it. However, to correct this problem, you will have to back up all programs and data, completely re-low-level format the drive, and use a drive translation method to reinterpret the drive cylinder and head count so that NetWare and DOS see it as having fewer than 1024 cylinders. You will have to use either third-party software or the hard drive controller manufacturer's low-level formatting program to put drive translation into effect. (You usually need to set jumpers on the controller as well.) Of course, you must then reinstall NetWare on the hard drive using ELSGEN for ELS NetWare or NETGEN for NetWare 2.1X, and restore all your programs and data. Netware 2.2 does not have a problem with drives over 1024 cylinders. Even though you may see a message on boot up that says "WARNING! Could not read bad block table" on the file server console, you can safely ignore it and the file server will function properly, this message simply means the cold boot loader has acknowledged that the drive exceeds 1024 cylinders.

Symptom

You receive the file server error message "Stack overflow detected by kernel" and the file server abends.

Probable Cause

A memory failure or overflow in file server RAM caused by a corrupted OS, poor power conditioning, or a RAM chip problem shuts down the server.

Solution

Reboot the file server. If the problem persists, run a memory test program such as CheckIt on the file server to identify bad RAM. Replace the indicated bad RAM chips.

Symptom

You receive an "NMI interrupt" or a "Parity error" error message at the file server and the file server abends, causing a fatal error that shuts down the server.

Probable Cause

The CPU received a pulse on its non-maskable interrupt line, indicating a problem with RAM. This may have been caused by a hardware failure, poor power line conditioning, or a corrupted NET$OS.EXE operating system file.

Solution

First, reboot the file server. NMI and parity errors are often transient and simply rebooting the computer will clear them. If the error persists, reinstall the operating system with NETGEN -C (NetWare 2.1*X*) or INSTALL -M -L (NetWare 2.2). If the problem continues, run a memory test program such as CheckIt on the file server to identify bad

Symptom

You receive the error message "Bad block returned via Free" or "Invalid process ID passed by interrupt procedure to kernel" at the file server console. The file server abends and shuts down.

Probable Cause

In the first case, a block of memory returned from a process to the DGROUP memory pool overlaps a portion of RAM not allocated. In the second case, an interrupt procedure passed a message to a process not defined in the kernel.

Solution

Reboot the file server. If the error occurs again, replace RAM or check power quality coming into the file server (see the next section, "AC Power and UPS Monitoring").

Symptom

You receive the message "*** WARNING *** ACTIVE FILES OPEN. HALT NETWORK?" when you type **down** at the file server console.

Probable Cause

You typed **down** but at least one workstation still had files open on the file server or a workstation was powered off without the user first logging out.

Solution

Type **n** to answer no, and then have all users close their files and log out at their workstations. If a workstation has crashed, use the CLEAR STATION command at the file

server or, at a workstation, type fconsole and choose
Connection Information, Current Connections. Highlight
the connection and press the DEL key to clear the
connection and to close the workstation's files. If there is
no response from the file server keyboard or you cannot log
in to run FCONSOLE, type y to answer yes to halt the
network. In this case you could lose some data.

➤   *Tech tip:*   *Changed information in open data files is*
normally written from the file server cache buffers to the
hard disk every three seconds. The DOWN command writes
out those cache buffers, closes open files, updates the FAT
and directory tables, and shuts down the operating system
in preparation for turning off power at the file server.

Symptom

You cannot add or delete users or groups from the bindery
in SYSCON. When you try, you get an error message or no
response. You also cannot change your password or use
the CAPTURE command.

Probable Cause

The bindery is corrupted.

Solution

Log in as supervisor. Type cd\system. Type bindfix. This
executes the BINDFIX.EXE program, which will examine
the bindery files NET$BIND.SYS and NET$BVAL.SYS and
attempt to fix any corruption problems. BINDFIX creates
two files named NET$BIND.OLD and NET$BVAL.OLD as it
runs. In case BINDFIX does not successfully complete its
bindery check, you can type bindrest to restore the
information from these .OLD files and return the system to
its previous state. You are no better off than you were
before, but you at least still have access to the system. You

can then try restoring the bindery from a backup or down the server and run VREPAIR.

AC Power and UPS Monitoring

Like workstations, file servers are susceptible to AC power blackouts, brownouts, spikes, and surges (see Chapter 5, "Workstation Hardware"). Unlike workstations, if such problems occur on a file server, the entire network is affected, causing conditions ranging from a momentary glitch to a fatal abend. Nearly all file servers installed today are therefore plugged in to an uninterruptible power supply (UPS) to ensure an ongoing supply of AC power to the system in the event of power company problems or power transmission line failure.

The basic off-line or switching UPS is designed to switch from AC to battery power when commercial power drops below a certain voltage level or fails altogether. The better switching UPSs also filter and regulate AC power so that the file server receives steady and clean voltage levels. The very best UPSs are the on-line variety that continuously converts commercial AC power to DC power to keep the battery charged. This type of UPS completely isolates the file server from commercial power and its potential fluctuations.

A good UPS is a small investment to make in order to prevent a sudden loss of power to the server. Prices today range anywhere from $500 to $5000, depending on the length of battery life and the output wattage of the UPS. However, by itself, an on-line off-line UPS is still not sufficient protection for the file server from AC power failure. To more adequately prevent power problems from affecting file server performance, make an investment in an "intelligent" on-line or off-line UPS that can work with a

UPS monitoring card installed in the file server. This can be a stand-alone card, a serial keycard or disk coprocessor board (DCB) with UPS monitoring built in, or the mouse port on a PS/2. This monitoring device works in conjunction with the NetWare operating system to warn users when AC power goes off and the UPS switches to battery backup. The monitoring system transmits a warning message to all active workstations and then, after several minutes, automatically issues a "down" command at the file server to effect an orderly, automatic, and unattended shutdown of the server.

Without UPS monitoring, it is possible for AC power to go off, the UPS to switch on and, if no one responds to the warning light or alarm on the UPS, after the battery drains, for the file server to simply stop. This can in turn result in file allocation table and directory errors, operating system problems, and corruption of application programs or database files.

Symptom

You receive the error message "Invalid configuration in the CONFIG.UPS (2.1 NetWare) or SERVER.CFG (2.12, 2.15, or NetWare 2.2) file" or "Invalid config parameter in the CONFIG.UPS (2.1 NetWare) or SERVER.CFG (2.12, 2.15, or NetWare 2.2) file" when the file server boots up.

Probable Cause

When you typed the UPS monitoring setup commands you made a mistake, or the file is corrupted. This error is not fatal but UPS monitoring will not be established.

Solution

The CONFIG.UPS or SHELL.CFG files are simply ASCII text files created in the SYSTEM directory of volume SYS on the file server. They can be edited with any DOS text editor

such as EDLIN. Edit the appropriate file so the parameters
are correct, and then down the file server and reboot it.

➤ *Tech tip:* **Make sure you type commands in these files in
uppercase only. The "Supervisor's Reference" and
"Supervisor's Guide" (2.1X) and "Using the Network" (2.2)
manuals provide the syntax for creating these files.
However, you also must consult the manual that came with
your particular UPS and UPS monitoring card to make sure
you have the correct settings for the type of UPS monitoring
board and the time-out switches for AC power and
battery-low warnings.**

Symptom

All workstations receive the message "Batteries are low.
Server will go down in # minutes."

Probable Cause

The UPS has gone to battery backup because of AC power
failure. However, the charge in the batteries is almost gone
and UPS monitoring is about to down the file server in
response.

Solution

Log out all stations immediately so that data is not lost
when the server is shut down. Reboot the file server when
normal AC power is restored.

4

Workstation Bootup and NetWare Shell Issues

The vast majority of workstations on NOVELL networks run MS- or PC-DOS as their operating system. DOS must load its system files into RAM before other programs, including the NetWare routing and shell files, load. The DOS system files can take up anywhere from 60K to 128K of RAM, depending on the version of DOS being used. (The recent release of DOS 5.0 provides the means to load much of DOS into what is called "high RAM," thereby freeing up more of the precious 640K of base memory in the workstation.)

Most NOVELL networks use the NetWare routing file IPX.COM and the shell file NET3.COM, NET4.COM, or NET5.COM. IPX stands for Internetwork Packet Exchange, and it is the file that sets up communication between the NetWare shell and the physical network board installed in the workstation. As such, it must be configured to match the network board manufacturer's specifications and to avoid hardware conflicts with other devices in the workstation.

The NETX.COM file is the NetWare shell, which translates DOS and application commands into NetWare commands. Both of these files are discussed further in this chapter and in Chapter 5, "Workstation Hardware."

The problems that can develop from the inability of the workstation to properly load DOS, configure the DOS environment once it is loaded, or properly load in the routing and shell files, are covered in the following discussion. In addition, you will find in this chapter

sections dealing with common OS/2, Windows 3.0, and
Macintosh problems since, although these operating
system environments are not yet as widespread as DOS,
they are gaining ground daily on the dominance of DOS as
the preferred workstation operating system environment.

DOS System Files

There are two MS-DOS system files, named IO.SYS and
MSDOS.SYS (PC-DOS names them IBMBIO.COM and
IBMDOS.COM), that are marked Hidden System and Read
Only in the root directory of the workstation boot disk.
Along with COMMAND.COM, these files are required to
boot up the workstation. If these files become corrupted or
are deleted, the user will not be able to get a DOS
prompt—A:\ if the workstation boots from a floppy disk or
C:\ if the workstation boots from a hard disk.

Symptom

The user receives a "Non-system disk or disk error" error
message when he or she attempts to boot up the
workstation. The workstation stops and cannot load
network routing or shell files.

Probable Cause

The hidden system files have become corrupted or have
been deleted.

Solution

If the workstation is using a floppy disk for bootup, take the
disk to a machine with a hard drive using the same version
of DOS, and type **SYS A:** at the C:\ prompt. You should

see the message "System transferred." Return to the
workstation you took this disk from and attempt to boot up
on the network.

Tech tip: *This floppy disk is configured for the specific
hardware in the workstation and may not work correctly in
a different workstation (see the section entitled "IPX" later
in this chapter).*

If the workstation is using a hard drive for bootup, boot
from drive A with a DOS disk that is the same version as
the one being used on the hard drive (check versions by
making sure the file called COMMAND.COM in the root
directory of the hard drive matches the date and size of the
COMMAND.COM file on the boot disk you are using in
drive A). At the A:\ prompt, type `SYS C:`, and you should
see the "System transferred" message. You should now be
able to boot from drive C onto the network.

Further Help

If the user continues to get boot error messages at the
workstation, you may need to consult the DOS manual and
run FDISK to ensure the partition on the hard drive is still
active. The system files might be in perfect condition, but
if the partition is no longer active or the bootstrap routine
on cylinder 0 has been corrupted, the user will still get an
error message. (The partition identifies how the hard disk is
divided—that is, drive C, D, or E. The first partition (C)
must be marked active when you run FDISK or the hard
disk will not boot. Both the partition and the boot sector,
which calls up the DOS hidden system files, exist on the
very first track of the hard disk, usually referred to as
cylinder 0.) Your last resort is to use third-party utilities
such as Norton Utilities to try to make the disk bootable
(run Norton Disk Doctor and choose Make a Disk Bootable).

DOS COMMAND.COM

COMMAND.COM is the DOS command interpreter located in the root directory of the boot disk that controls, among other things, keyboard input. If COMMAND.COM becomes corrupted or deleted, the user will again not be able to get a DOS prompt, and not be able to access the network. In addition, since COMMAND.COM must be available at all times to application programs for them to properly load into memory, run, and then exit from memory, a pointer to it is created in a small part of RAM called the DOS environment; this pointer tells application programs where to find COMMAND.COM.

The workstation needs a similar pointer for DOS to find its external program files. You create a path in DOS and assign a search drive in NetWare to create this pointer. This pointer then tells the operating system where to look for files stored on the file server hard disk that the user wants to access but that are not in the subdirectory in which the user is located.

Symptom

The user receives a "Bad or missing command interpreter" on bootup and the workstation locks up.

Probable Cause

COMMAND.COM has been deleted or corrupted.

Solution

Copy the same version of COMMAND.COM as was originally loaded on the workstation from a DOS boot disk to the hard drive if the workstation is booting from a hard drive, or from the C:\DOS directory of a hard drive to the floppy boot disk if the workstation does not have a hard drive. You should then be able to reboot the workstation onto the network without a problem.

Symptom

The user receives an "Incorrect version of DOS" or "Mismatch between DOS environment and network shell search mappings" error message when he or she attempts to execute a DOS command.

Probable Cause

The version of DOS the user booted up with does not match the version of DOS installed on the network, or the search path environment setting to the DOS files is incorrect.

Solution

Log in as supervisor and map a search drive to DOS in the system login script by using the variable statement

MAP INS S2:=SYS:PUBLIC\%machine\%os\%os_version

Next, build a subdirectory structure under the PUBLIC directory that looks like this:

F:\PUBLIC\IBM_PC\MSDOS\V3.30

If you have workstations using more than one version of DOS, then include, for example, V3.31, V4.01, V5.0, and so on, as subdirectories under MS-DOS. Finally, copy into each subdirectory all of the DOS files for each version being used on the network. NetWare will automatically match the version of COMMAND.COM booted to the correct subdirectory in the variable statement and use that version of DOS for all DOS external program calls and for all COMSPEC references (see the following symptom).

Symptom

The user exits from an application program and the error message "Insert disk with COMMAND.COM in the A drive and strike any key when ready" or "Invalid COMMAND.COM—Cannot load COMMAND, System Halted" appears. In the first case, the user must find a boot disk with a matching COMMAND.COM, and in the second case, the user must reboot the workstation.

Probable Cause

The workstation has no environment setting that tells the application program where to find COMMAND.COM once it finishes executing.

Solution

Log in as supervisor and place a statement in the system login script that tells network programs and applications where to find COMMAND.COM so they can reload it after they have run. The statement COMSPEC=S2:COMMAND.COM is commonly placed in the System login script where the second search drive (S2) points to the DOS subdirectory from which COMMAND.COM should be reloaded.

➤ *Tech tip: It is best to set up the network this way and to avoid either having no COMSPEC statement in the login script or using a SET COMSPEC=A:\COMMAND.COM statement in the AUTOEXEC.BAT file when the workstation is booting from a floppy disk. In either case, the boot disk with COMMAND.COM on it must be in drive A when you exit from the application program. Otherwise, the workstation will hang with the preceding error message and you will not be able to exit to the menu or prompt until the boot disk is replaced in drive A.*

CONFIG.SYS

The CONFIG.SYS file is the system configuration file that allows the workstation to load into the DOS environment special commands and software programs, called drivers, that customize DOS to fit the particular needs of the workstation and the special devices that may have been added to it, such as a mouse, an expanded memory card, an external floppy disk drive, and so on. This file has become increasingly important on NetWare workstations since it can severely impact network performance if command lines used in it have parameters that are not set correctly or load in conflicting memory-resident programs (TSRs) or device drivers.

Symptom

The user gets a "Not enough files open" error message when the workstation loads an application program, or the application program loads fine but hangs or runs very slowly when it does run.

Probable Cause

After the system files load, DOS looks for a CONFIG.SYS file with statements that further set up the DOS environment. The FILES= statement and BUFFERS= statement usually found in this file have no bearing on the network per se. (The network equivalent for the CONFIG.SYS file is the SHELL.CFG or NET.CFG file.) However, if you load any application from your local hard disk, these statements do affect the environment and, if they are set too low, cause errors or very slow performance.

Solution

Place a statement that says FILES=40 in the workstation's CONFIG.SYS file. This opens up 40 local file handles for

DOS. If the workstation is running Windows 3.0 or DESQview, this should be increased to FILES=60. Use a BUFFERS=20 statement to avoid slow performance or hanging of application programs.

➤   *Tech tip: Use any DOS text editor to edit the CONFIG.SYS file and remember the user must reboot the workstation after you change the CONFIG.SYS file for any changes you make to take effect.*

Symptom

The user receives one of two possible error messages, either "Out of room in the environment space" or "Insufficient space in DOS environment to add new search mappings," and the application or utility program does not run.

Probable Cause

This message refers to the amount of space reserved by DOS for system and program environmental parameters. The default on any 3.*X* and 4.*X* version of DOS is 160 bytes (DOS 5.0 is 256 bytes). If the workstation uses more bytes in the statement lines in the CONFIG.SYS and AUTOEXEC.BAT files that set up the environment than are available, the user will receive this error message either on bootup or when he or she attempts to load your application into RAM.

Solution

Edit the workstation's CONFIG.SYS file to include the statement

SHELL=C:\ *(or A:\)* COMMAND.COM /P /E:512

(You can go up to 32K if you wish, but 512 bytes is usually sufficient.)

Symptom

The user sees an error message flash by quickly on the screen as he or she boots up that says a particular file is "Bad or missing." Then, a hardware device such as the mouse will not work.

Probable Cause

The workstation does not give the correct path in the CONFIG.SYS file to the location of the device driver trying to load.

Solution

Check the path statements to the device drivers. For instance, a statement such as DEVICE=C:\MOUSE\ MOUSE.SYS allows DOS to find and load the driver file for the mouse if it is being stored in a subdirectory called C:\MOUSE.

➤ *Tech tip: If the workstation has a mouse, check the documentation that came with the mouse to make sure the correct driver is loading (many mouse drivers now load as .COM files from the AUTOEXEC.BAT file and do not use the CONFIG.SYS file).*

Symptom

The user receives the error message "Invalid drive specification" as the workstation tries to boot up onto the file server.

Probable Cause

There is a statement in the CONFIG.SYS file that says LASTDRIVE=Z. This is most commonly found on workstations that were previously stand-alone machines with hard drives in which the user wanted to use the DOS SUBST command to substitute logical drive letters for subdirectory paths. NetWare, however, uses this command to select the next available DOS drive letter for the first mapped network drive. Since there is no letter available after Z, the error message occurs.

Solution

The vast majority of networks use drive F as the first network drive. It therefore makes sense to set this parameter to LASTDRIVE=E for most workstations.

AUTOEXEC.BAT

The AUTOEXEC.BAT file automatically executes once DOS sees that it is there and runs any DOS or program commands that are typed in.

Place commands in this file that load TSRs, set your prompt and path, possibly set up mouse and Windows configurations, and load the NetWare protocol driver (IPX) and the NetWare shell (NET#—where # is the number of the version of DOS running at the workstation: 2, 3, 4, or 5). Keep the AUTOEXEC.BAT file as standardized as you can for all workstations on the network to avoid time-consuming maintenance problems.

Symptom

A "Bad command or file name" error message flashes by on the screen on bootup and the user cannot log in to the file server.

Probable Cause

One or more statements in the AUTOEXEC.BAT file do not correctly point to where the executable files being called for are located.

Solution

Edit the AUTOEXEC.BAT file and correct the statement. For example, if IPX.COM is stored in a subdirectory called C:\NET, the AUTOEXEC.BAT file should have a line in it that says C:\NET\IPX, rather than simply IPX.

➤ *Tech tip: Make sure the AUTOEXEC.BAT file also loads executable files in the correct order. First, set the PROMPT to PG (better here than in the System login script since, if the user does not get access to the file server, the System login script will, of course, not run, and the user may end up at a confusing A>, C>, or F> prompt). Next, load TSRs (if you must load them at all). Make sure the AUTOEXEC.BAT file then loads IPX and the version of the NetWare shell being used (typically NET3, NET4, or NET5, depending on the version of DOS). You should then be able to have F: and LOGIN as the last two commands so that the user ends up with a network prompt asking for a login name. This is an example of a very basic but effective AUTOEXEC.BAT file to automate the NetWare login procedure:*

```
ECHO OFF
CLS
PROMPT $P$G
IPX
NET3     (If the workstation is using DOS 3.X)
NETBIOS  (Only if required by the application)
INT2F    (Only if required by the application)
F:
LOGIN    (servername/username)
```

Symptom

The user attempts to execute an application program and it indicates it will not run unless NETBIOS is loaded first.

Probable Cause

Some older network applications; diagnostic, E-mail, and gateway programs; and many Windows 3.0 programs require emulation of IBM's NetBIOS connector and the PC LAN program.

Solution

Edit the AUTOEXEC.BAT file at the workstation to load the NETBIOS.EXE file generated with IPX during WSGEN (or SHGEN in V2.1X) and the INT2F.COM file.

➤ *Tech tip: For a full description of the WSGEN and SHGEN IPX generation process, consult your NetWare 2.2 "Installing and Maintaining the Network" manual or your NetWare 2.1X "Installation" manual (also see following sections on these topics).*

Further Help

The various NETBIOS value statements, and common NETBIOS error messages associated with NOVELL's implementation of NetBIOS, can be found in the *NetWare Workstation Troubleshooting and Maintenance Handbook* by Edward Liebing, Charles D. Knutson, and Michael Day (LAN TIMES/McGraw-Hill, 1990) and the NetWare 2.2 "Using the Network" manual.

Symptom

The user types a command or executes a menu selection and a wrong or unexpected program executes, or the user gets an "Invalid drive in search path" error message.

Probable Cause

The workstation has a path statement in the AUTOEXEC.BAT file. The path statement here executes before NetWare's login scripts and automatically adds each subdirectory to which the workstation has set a path as a NetWare separate search drive statement at the end of the login script drive mappings. This may cause search conflicts or cause unwanted single-user utilities or other programs to run on the network.

Solution

Map search drives with the NetWare MAP command in a login script if you wish the user to have search drive pointers to local hard drive subdirectories. For example:

MAP INS S16:=C:*myprog*

➤ *Tech tip:* **Make sure the user then reboots the workstation each time after he or she logs out from the network and before logging in again to keep the search environment clean.**

Symptom

The user exits from an application program and receives a "Cannot load COMMAND.COM" or "Insert disk with COMMAND.COM" error message; the menu hangs; if the user tries to log out or run any NetWare menu or command-line utilities or DOS external commands, he or she receives a "Bad command or file name" error message.

Probable Cause

The user ran the AUTOEXEC.BAT file after having logged in to the network. The PATH statement in the AUTOEXEC.BAT file then executes, bumping all NetWare search drive mappings to regular drive mappings. The user can no longer access any executable files previously mapped in search drives to subdirectories on the network, including the DOS, PUBLIC, and LOGIN directories.

Solution

Have the user change into the PUBLIC or LOGIN directory (type **CD\PUBLIC**) and log in again (type **LOGIN** *username*). This procedure resets search drive mappings. Alternatively, type **LOGOUT**, reboot the workstation, and log in again.

➤ *Tech tip:* *If the user does not understand what has happened and continues to use the AUTOEXEC.BAT file to restart a local menu, this can become an ongoing and frustrating problem.*

IPX

Internetwork Packet Exchange (IPX) is the protocol driver for NetWare, generated by using WSGEN in NetWare 2.2 and SHGEN in Netware 2.1*X* to create the file IPX.COM. This file loads into DOS and creates the interface between the NetWare shell and the network LAN board installed in the workstation. Thus, if a NOVELL NE2000 Ethernet network board is installed in the workstation, you must generate an IPX.COM file using the NE2000 configuration driver files supplied by NOVELL. Vendors other than NOVELL will ship the configuration driver files for their network boards with the boards.

You must then follow the instructions for using WSGEN in the Netware 2.2 "Installing and Maintaining the Network" manual or for using SHGEN in the Netware 2.1*X* "Installation" manual, in order to generate the correct IPX.COM file for whichever network board you are using. IPX.COM may not load properly and establish connection with the network board in the workstation for several reasons.

Symptom

An error message appears indicating the network board failed to "Initialize," or the workstation may simply appear to hang.

Probable Cause

The option chosen to configure the board does not match the board's IRQ, base memory, or base I/O address.

Solution

You have two choices if there is a mismatch. First, you can change the hardware settings on the network board to match the IPX configuration. Reboot the workstation with DOS, locate the IPX.COM file, and type IPX I to check the configuration of this file. Next, locate the manual that came with the network board in the workstation, open the workstation, and make sure the dip switches and jumpers on the network board are set to match the configuration of the IPX.COM file.

➤ *Tech tip: If the workstation is a PS/2 or EISA bus machine, reload the reference or configuration disk to check and reprogram the network board configuration (see the manual for the particular machine for the steps to do this).*

Second, and this is usually easier, you can use the utility program DCONFIG located on the NetWare 2.2 WSGEN disk or the NetWare 2.1*X* SHGEN -1 disk. Type DCONFIG IPX.COM to see the options available. The option that has an asterisk (*) next to it is currently in use. To change the option so it matches the network board switch and jumper settings, type DCONFIG IPX.COM SHELL:,# where # is the option number matching the board in the workstation. Reboot the workstation and try to load IPX.COM again.

You may also use the IPX /O option to select a different configuration; for example, IPX /O4 selects configuration 4. Or you can place a CONFIG OPTION = # statement in the SHELL.CFG or NET.CFG file, where # is the option number you wish to load. Both of these command-line switches are simply alternatives to DCONFIG as a means to change the IRQ, base I/O, and base memory address choice for a board you have changed hardware settings on or newly installed in the workstation. Unlike DCONFIG, these command-line switches do not make the change "stick" in the IPX file.

➤   *Tech tip:*   *If you are using one of the latest drivers that currently ship with NetWare 2.2, or a third-party driver that is "jumpers compatible," you have an even wider range of choices than the option numbers you can select using DCONFIG since you can use the new utility JUMPERS.EXE. This utility, located on the NETWARE 2.2 WSGEN disk, permits customizing the IPX.COM file for any combination of IRQ, base I/O, and base memory addresses required. You can even use JUMPERS to change the packet size IPX sends out on the cable. If you wish to copy JUMPERS to the disk the IPX.COM file is on in order to use it, make sure you copy over the files JUMPERS.HLP and SYS$MSG.DAT as well, or JUMPERS will not work.*

Symptom

You configure IPX.COM to match the workstation's network board configuration and IPX now loads properly. However, when NET# attempts to load, the user receives a "File server cannot be found" error message.

Probable Cause

Other hardware devices (mouse, modem, VGA card, printer, and so on) in the workstation are using the same

IRQ, base I/O, or base memory address as the network board.

Solution

Reconfigure the IPX.COM file and the switch and jumper settings on the network board to avoid conflicts with other devices, or remove the device that conflicts with the network board if there are no alternative nonconflicting options. If you still have problems, try replacing the network board since it probably has a hardware problem.

Symptom

You replace a network board with a new model or with a board from a different manufacturer. Now IPX "cannot initialize the LAN card at the workstation."

Probable Cause

New or different boards often require running WSGEN (2.2) or SHGEN (2.1X) to reconfigure and relink a new IPX.COM file. (DCONFIG and JUMPERS only change existing options; they cannot be used to generate a new IPX.COM.)

Solution

Run WSGEN as outlined in the NetWare 2.2 "Installing and Maintaining the Network" manual or SHGEN as outlined in the NetWare 2.1X "Installation" or "Maintenance" manual. Copy the newly generated IPX.COM file from the WSGEN directory in 2.2, or download it before you exit SHGEN in 2.1X, to the workstation boot disk.

Further Help

Most software drivers shipped with network boards have a README file on the disk that further explains the generation process for that particular board.

Symptom

The user gets the error message "IPX/SPX already loaded" when he or she types IPX at the command line.

Probable Cause

IPX can be loaded only one time into workstation RAM.

Solution

Have the user reboot the workstation before attempting to reload IPX.

Symptom

The user receives the message "IPX has not been loaded. Please load and then run the shell."

Probable Cause

The user attempted to load NET# before loading IPX.

Solution

Load IPX before NET# in the AUTOEXEC.BAT file.

ODI

The open data-link interface (ODI) is NOVELL's newest strategy for supporting multiple network protocols and drivers over a single network board. ODI creates a "logical" network board that can then send different packet types over one physical board and wire. This makes it possible to have, for instance, a PC using DOS share the same Ethernet cabling wire as a Macintosh or a UNIX-based workstation. ODI is thus a very flexible interface, but it is more complicated to set up than IPX.

Symptom

The NetWare ODI driver will not work with the network board in the workstation or will not load properly. The user receives a "Cannot initialize LAN card" or "Not ODI compatible" error message.

Probable Cause

For ODI to work, you must use the ODI driver files found in the DOSODI subdirectory on the NetWare 2.2 WSGEN disk. (ODI was not shipped with 2.1X NetWare.) Not all boards will work with these driver files, but NOVELL has provided drivers for many common boards such as the NOVELL NE2000, the 3COM 3C503, and standard ARCnet and Token-Ring boards.

Solution

Purchase an ODI-compatible board and follow the instructions in the NetWare 2.2 "Installing and Maintaining the Network" manual for loading the ODI drivers. Make sure you use a DOS text editor to create a NET.CFG file that looks like this:

```
read only compatibility=on
link driver NE2000    (or the driver needed)
INT 4                 (or whichever interrupt
                       can be used)
```

Then create an AUTOEXEC.BAT file that, in order, loads LSL.COM, the LAN driver file, the protocol interface file (such as IPXODI.COM), and the NetWare shell. For example:

```
LSL
NE2000
IPXODI
NET3
```

Remote Boot

A diskless workstation is a workstation that does not boot from a floppy disk or hard drive, but instead boots from a programmable read only memory chip (PROM) installed on the network board. Almost all network board manufacturers provide a socket on their boards for plugging in such a remote boot PROM, although most manufacturers require you to order the PROM separately. Once it is installed, you will need to generate a remote boot image file with the DOSGEN utility located in the SYS:SYSTEM directory. This file is created and remains in the SYS:LOGIN directory on the file server, and it is the file the PROM looks for when it initiates the boot sequence at the workstation.

Symptom

The user receives error messages such as "A file server could not be found," "Invalid drive," or "Bad command or file name," and cannot access the file server.

Probable Cause

As supervisor, you did not correctly create the NET$DOS.SYS file in the SYS:LOGIN directory on every file server you wish users to log in to from remote boot workstations.

Solution

Follow the detailed steps for creating a remote boot image file provided in the NetWare 2.2 "Using the Network" and "Concepts" manuals and the NetWare 2.1X "Supervisor's Guide."

➤ Tech tip: Make sure to flag NET$DOS.SYS Shareable after it has been created if more than one workstation will be

*accessing it. Copy the AUTOEXEC.BAT file you are using
to both the SYS:LOGIN directory and each user's default
home directory to avoid a "Batch file missing" error
message.*

Read the NetWare manual instructions very carefully and
follow them exactly during the more complicated process
of creating multiple remote boot image files, paying
particular attention to the creation of the BOOTCONF.SYS
file.

Finally, make sure you have properly installed the remote
boot PROM in your workstation network board and set
jumpers or dip switches correctly on the board to activate
the PROM (see Chapter 5, "Workstation Hardware").

Shell Versions

The NetWare shell intercepts DOS function calls from an
application and sends appropriate calls to the NetWare file
server. The shell is loaded into a DOS workstation after
IPX.COM.

NetWare 2.2 has increased the options available for
NetWare shells by providing, in addition to NET#.COM,
EMSNET#.EXE, which loads into expanded memory, and
XMSNET#.EXE, which loads into extended memory. (It is
also possible to use these new shell versions with NetWare
2.1X if you have the Windows utilities upgrade package
with the new 3.01e or 3.02 shell.) The new shells appear to
work fine in most machines, although both EMSNET# and
XMSNET# run more slowly than NET# loaded into high
memory with a third-party utility such as Quarterdeck's
QEMM.SYS.

Symptom

The user receives "A file server could not be found" error message or the shell hangs after being loaded into RAM.

Probable Cause

The shell could not attach to any file servers.

Solution

Have the user reboot the workstation from power off/on, or use the Reset button if the computer has one. (Sometimes, CTRL-ALT-DEL will not work because the processor does not reinitialize the network board.) If this fails, check to see if other workstations are able to log in to the file server. If other workstations are receiving the same error message, you are probably experiencing either a cabling problem (see Chapter 6, "Cabling") or a file server or external router problem (see Chapter 3, "The File Server").

If the error is specific to one workstation and it continues, reload a known good working shell onto that workstation boot disk to make sure the shell is not corrupted.

If the error persists, check the IPX file configuration, the network board (see Chapter 5, "Workstation Hardware"), and the cable connector (see Chapter 6, "Cabling") at the workstation.

Symptom

The user receives the error message "Not running on top of DOS version #."

Probable Cause

The shell the workstation is using does not match the version of DOS booted with.

Solution

Type Net# I at the workstation's boot disk prompt and
make sure the shell being used matches the version of DOS
being run. Replace the shell with the correct shell version.

Symptom

The user receives a "You are not connected to any file
servers" or "Connection is no longer valid" error message.

Probable Cause

The user has been working on the network but now there
is a conflict between the shell and a memory-resident
program (TSR), the shell has been corrupted, the cabling
system has failed, or the file server has gone down.

Solution

If other workstations are also receiving error messages the
problem is cabling (see Chapter 6, "Cabling") or file server
related (see Chapter 3, "The File Server"). If only one
workstation is having trouble, reboot the workstation from
power off/on to clear RAM and reinitialize the network
board. If the problem persists, remove all TSRs from the
workstation's CONFIG.SYS or AUTOEXEC.BAT file and
reboot.

If the problem continues, reload a known good working
shell onto the workstation's boot disk to make sure the
shell is not corrupted.

The last step is to replace the IPX file, the network board
(see Chapter 5, "Workstation Hardware"), or the cable
connector (see Chapter 6, "Cabling") at the workstation.

Symptom

The user attaches to the wrong file server and gets an "Access denied" error message when he or she attempts to log in.

Probable Cause

The shell has issued a "Get nearest server" message and has attached to the first available file server, but not one for which the user has a viable login name or password.

Solution

Include a LOGIN *servername\username* statement in the workstation's AUTOEXEC.BAT file to specify the server you wish the user to log in to. Alternatively, include a PREFERRED SERVER = *servername* statement in the SHELL.CFG or NET.CFG file so the shell does not simply "get" the nearest (next available) file server but rather attaches to the specified preferred file server where the user has the correct login name and password and rights assignments. You can also accomplish this by adding a /PS=*servername* switch after Net# in the AUTOEXEC.BAT file.

➤   *Tech tip: The SHELL.CFG or NET.CFG file is used to modify the shell defaults. When IPX and NET# load, they check for the existence of these files and use the statements in them to modify default settings. Following are some of the most common problems that can be corrected by modifying the SHELL.CFG or NET.CFG file on the workstation's boot disk.*

Symptom

The user receives the error message "Not enough SPX connections available."

Probable Cause

The workstation requires more SPX connections available to perform the operations of the application program being used at the workstation. This is commonly a problem with workstations being used as print servers (see Chapter 2, "Printing").

Solution

Include a statement in the SHELL.CFG or NET.CFG file that says SPX CONNECTIONS = 60 (or more if needed in increments of 10).

Symptom

The error message "Not enough file handles available" or "Unable to open a file" appears at the workstation.

Probable Cause

The workstation does not have enough network file handles available for the application or utility program running at the workstation. Many programs that use large numbers of windows (such as Microsoft Windows 3.0) or screen masks (large accounting or database programs) require more than the default 40 file server file handles available to the shell.

Solution

Include a FILE HANDLES = # statement in the SHELL.CFG or NET.CFG file when the number of file handles open on the file server needs to be over the default of 40. Check the application program manuals for this specification.

➤ *Tech tip: If you increase the number of file handles in the SHELL.CFG or NET.CFG files, make sure you go back and edit the CONFIG.SYS file so the FILE= statement matches this number.*

Symptom

The workstation is a Compaq computer booting with Compaq DOS and the user gets an "Incorrect version of DOS" or "Bad or missing command interpreter" error message.

Probable Cause

The user does not have the correct search drive mapping and COMSPEC setting in their user login script for Compaq DOS.

Solution

Include a LONG MACHINE TYPE = COMPAQ statement in the workstation's SHELL.CFG or NET.CFG file. You will then need to create this subdirectory structure on the file server:

F:\PUBLIC\COMPAQ\PCDOS*v2.x or 3.x*

Symptom

The user's application program crashes when he or she tries to run it, possibly returning a "critical error" message such as "Cannot open a file" or "Cannot write to a file."

Probable Cause

In versions of NetWare earlier than 2.1, the Read Only flag permitted application programs write access. NetWare 2.1*X*, 2.2, and 3.11 do not, and application program files flagged Read Only will truly prevent the application from writing back to them.

Solution

In the NET.CFG or SHELL.CFG file at the workstation, include a READ ONLY COMPATIBILITY = ON statement

for applications that require read/write access to their
program files that have been flagged Read Only.

NetWare Versions

NOVELL's recent release of NetWare 2.2 provides the
opportunity to migrate to a version of NetWare that is
easier to install and maintain. This upgrade path requires
loading a new operating system, new system files, and
new public utility files on to the 2.1X file server using the
NetWare 2.2 INSTALL program, in order to make use of the
new Netware 2.2 utilities (see the NetWare 2.2 "Installing
and Maintaining the Network" manual).

Symptom

The user "attaches" to a 2.2 or 3.11 file server after logging
in to a 2.1X file server and receives NetWare error
messages when he or she attempts to run common
NetWare utilities such as SYSCON or FILER on the newer
server. These error messages are usually in the form of a
full-screen display that appears as a "critical error"
message indicating the particular utility cannot be run.

Probable Cause

The workstation is using the old NET# shell (prior to the
version 3.01 release) when it boots up. The old NET# shell
works fine on the older version of NetWare but does not
work on the newer versions.

Solution

Since NOVELL has made an excellent effort to keep its
upgrades downwardly compatible, there will not be a
problem if the user logs in to the 2.2 file server first and

then attaches to the 2.1X file server. However, to ensure continuing compatibility across file servers on a multiple file server network or internetwork, copy the contents of the PUBLIC subdirectory on the file server running NetWare 2.2 to the PUBLIC subdirectories of any file servers on the network still running NetWare 2.1X.

The procedure is to log in to the NetWare 2.2 file server and then "attach" to the 2.1X file server (ATTACH *servername*). Map a drive to the SYS:PUBLIC directory on that file server:

MAP O:=*servername*\SYS:PUBLIC

Go to O: in this example and flag all files N (FLAG *.* N) for normal, which is Non-Shareable Read/Write. Then, at the O:\PUBLIC> prompt, ncopy all of the files from the PUBLIC subdirectory on the 2.2 file server into this subdirectory:

NCOPY 2.2*servername*\SYS:PUBLIC*.*

Finally, copy the new NET# shell on the 2.2 WSGEN disk onto all of the boot disks for the network.

➤ *Tech tip: You should also regenerate IPX with WSGEN and copy it onto the boot disks as well so the IPX version matches the shell version to avoid possible glitches and to use most of the new shell utilities.*

Memory Issues and Conflicts

Programs that terminate and stay resident (TSR) in memory can cause the workstation to hang when it attempts to load IPX or NET# or can cause later conflicts when application programs or NetWare utilities attempt to run. These programs do not automatically remove themselves from workstation memory and return the memory they were using to DOS for other programs to use. Instead, they remain in the memory address location they initially were assigned by DOS, and the user can free this memory only by rebooting the computer or through sophisticated use of memory-management utilities. It is a good idea to avoid using TSRs as much as possible since the conflicts and problems they can cause are often difficult to diagnose.

Symptom

The user receives an "Out of memory" error message or the program or utility locks up.

Probable Cause

The user installed a TSR from their login script or from the NOVELL MENU utility. Any TSR loaded from the login script or MENU utility will not unlock memory for other uses that was released by the login script or MENU utility when the user exited from it. There will now be a "hole" in memory that cannot be used by other programs or utilities. The 5K TSR could end up costing 50K of workstation RAM.

Solution

Have the user reboot the workstation (possibly corrupting program and data files on the file server or losing information in workstation RAM, but there is nothing else you can do). Try installing the TSR from the user's AUTOEXEC.BAT file before the user logs in to the network or from a batch file after the user exits from the login script and before he or she accesses the MENU utility. If the problem persists, change the order you load the TSR in relation to IPX or NET#. If problems still continue, do not load the TSR.

➤ *Tech tip: DOS 5.0 now includes a utility called MEM that allows you to see workstation memory usage. Other utilities, such as TurboPower Software's MAPMEM and Touchstone Software Corporation's CheckIt, have been around for quite some time for the same purpose.*

It is best to avoid the TSR problem altogether by loading as few TSRs at the workstation as possible, and only those critically needed for network performance, such as remote printing capability at the workstation.

Symptom

The user receives an "Out of memory" error message when an application attempts to load.

Probable Cause

The application is too big to reside in the 640K base memory area.

Solution

If the user has a 386-level workstation, use Quarterdeck's QEMM and OPTIMIZE programs (make sure you use version 5.1, which is compatible with Windows) to load both IPX and NET# into high memory (still a better choice than using EMSNET# or XMSNET#, which load only the shell high and which also slow workstation performance).

If the user has a 286-level workstation with at least a megabyte of RAM, use the new NOVELL XMSNET# shell and move the shell itself into higher memory. Used in combination with DOS 5.0's new capability to load most of DOS's internal commands and device drivers into high memory on either a 286 or 386 machine with extended memory, you can usually end up with 550K to 600K of base memory available at the workstation. (See the DOS 5.0 manual for the Loadhi procedure.)

OS/2

Operating System/2 problems differ substantially from DOS problems. Since OS/2 is a multitasking operating system capable of running multiple processes, it goes well beyond DOS in its requirements for setup and utilization. For a more complete description of OS/2 and its performance demands on a NOVELL network, see the *NetWare Workstation Troubleshooting and Maintenance Handbook* by Edward Liebing, Charles D. Knutson, and Michael Day (LAN TIMES/McGraw-Hill, 1990), as well as the documentation that comes with the OS/2 Requester software shipped by NOVELL. This writing predates the latest release of OS/2 V2.0, which may be available on or before this book's publication date, and that promises to address some of the following problems.

Symptom

OS/2 will not load and run on the workstation. The workstation starts to boot and then hangs.

Probable Cause

Unlike DOS, OS/2 is not a generic product. It requires an original equipment manufacturer (OEM) version that will run on a particular computer.

Solution

Make sure the user has the correct OEM version of OS/2. Check with the hardware vendor for compatibility with OS/2.

Symptom

OS/2 begins to load but then stops with an error of "System halted" or "File not found."

Probable Cause

OS/2 and the NetWare Requester require a series of device drivers loaded from the CONFIG.SYS file. The series is out of order or the CONFIG.SYS file is missing a driver.

Solution

Check the workstation's CONFIG.SYS file for errors: watch carefully as the CONFIG.SYS file loads into RAM for any "Could not load device driver" or "Could not find device driver" error messages as the CONFIG.SYS file runs. Note the error messages and fix the problem indicated. Make sure the CONFIG.PST file created by the NetWare Requester INSTALL program has been correctly patched into the CONFIG.SYS file, that the remarks (REM) notations are removed appropriately, and that the order of loading is correct.

➤   *Tech tip:* *It can be difficult to catch error messages in the CONFIG.SYS file since they scroll by very quickly, so you may need to stare hard and be ready to tap the* PAUSE *key on the keyboard very fast to try to capture the error message on the screen.*

Symptom

The workstation hard disk works very hard or "thrashes" as OS/2 applications run; the user experiences very slow performance or unpredictable workstation hangs.

Probable Cause

There is too little RAM installed at the workstation (4 megabytes is the absolute minimum, but more is needed if the user expects to multitask more than one or two programs) so the overflow from RAM must be swapped out to disk. Hangs or other problems occur when the operating system attempts to swap essentially nonswappable kernel areas of the OS/2 operating system out to disk.

Solution

Install more RAM in the workstation.

Symptom

The user receives an error message that the "LAN card failed to initialize."

Probable Cause

The workstation is not using the correct OS/2 LAN driver file.

Solution

Follow very carefully the procedures laid out during the OS/2 NetWare Requester installation process to select the correct LAN driver for the workstation network board being used.

Symptom

Network utilities located in the SYS:PUBLIC and LOGIN directories do not work.

Probable Cause

OS/2 utilities are not the same as DOS utilities in NetWare, but they are named the same. They therefore must be loaded into other directories on the SYS: volume of the file server.

Solution

Use the NetWare Requester utility installation program SERVINST.CMD to place the OS/2 utilities into the subdirectories SYS:PUBLIC\OS2 and SYS:LOGIN\OS2.

➤ *Tech tip:* **The program SERVINST can be run from either DOS or OS/2. Before running SERVINST at the A:\ prompt, map drive L to SYS:LOGIN\OS2 (A:\>MAP L:=servername**

*SYS:LOGIN\OS2) and drive P to SYS:PUBLIC\OS2 (A:\>MAP
P:=servername\SYS:PUBLIC\OS2). Make these permanent
mappings for the workstation in the user's login script (see
Chapter 1, "System Management").*

Symptom

The user cannot log in to the file server. He or she receives
an "Access denied" error message.

Probable Cause

The user is not attaching first to the file server with the
OS/2 utilities installed.

Solution

Install the OS/2 utilities on every file server to which the
user might attach. Alternatively, place the key OS/2
NetWare utilities (ATTACH, LOGIN, MAP, and SLIST) in
the local hard disk subdirectory the user boots from
(because of its 10-megabyte size, OS/2 demands
installation on and booting from a hard disk).

➤ *Tech tip: **It** is almost never a good idea to access a
NetWare file server from the OS/2 DOS compatibility box for
extensive application work. (OS/2 V2.0 promises to change
this limitation.) Although it may be a convenient means to
perform some simple system administration tasks, it is
cleaner and less problematic to simply reboot the
workstation with a DOS floppy disk (or use the dual boot
option if it is installed) if the user wishes to spend any time
at all on the network under DOS. This may, in fact, be a
requirement if the user is working with the high-
performance file system (HPFS) available with OS/2, which
is not DOS compatible.*

Further Help

The *NetWare Workstation Troubleshooting and Maintenance Handbook* by Edward Liebing, Charles D. Knutson, and Michael Day (LAN TIMES/McGraw-Hill, 1990) is an excellent source for very detailed information concerning OS/2 and the installation of the NetWare Requester for OS/2. The NetWare Requester error codes for OS/2 listed therein are cryptic at best but may help give you a direction to search in if you have further problems.

Microsoft Windows 3.0

Since Windows is an "operating environment" that controls some aspects of PC operations previously controlled by DOS, if Windows is not properly installed on the network, it may seriously degrade or even halt workstation performance. For instance, Windows can generate a packet transmission load on the wire sufficient to bring network performance to its knees, create "Network error sending on the network" error messages, hang the workstation, or cause other inexplicable errors. You can avoid many pitfalls by making sure you have the latest version of Windows, 3.0a (Windows 3.1 is in beta test at this time; it should be out by publication date and may reduce or eliminate some of the problems), the latest IPX drivers and NetWare Shell versions (3.01e or 3.02), the latest NetWare utilities, and are aware of the following potential problems.

Symptom

During the Windows SETUP procedure, the workstation generates the error message "Cannot create WIN.COM."

Probable Cause

The user ran SETUP /N with Windows files that have not been uncompressed.

Solution

Uncompress all the Windows files with the EXPAND.EXE program and run SETUP /N again.

➤ *Tech tip: It will not work to simply type "expand a:*.* f:\windows". As soon as the program finds a file on one of the Windows disks that is not compressed, it stops processing with a message that says the file is not compressed and will not process any other files on the disk following the uncompressed file in the directory order. To fix this problem, create the following EXPALL.BAT batch file recommended in the "Microsoft Windows User's Guide" in the F:\WINDOWS directory on the file server:*

```
a:
for %%i in (*.*) do f:\windows\expand %%i
   f:\windows\%%i
f:
```

Then, copy the program EXPAND.EXE into this subdirectory, insert the first Windows disk in drive A, and run the EXPALL batch file. Run the Windows SETUP /N program and then flag all files Shareable Read Only.

Symptom

The SETUP program hangs when loading at the workstation.

Probable Cause

There is a conflict between Windows, which uses the base I/O address 2E0h and the EMS page frame D0000-DFFFF, and the workstation's network board or VGA monitor.

Solution

Change the network board's base I/O address and base
memory address settings (see Chapter 5, "Workstation
Hardware," for how to resolve network board configuration
conflicts). You can also use the EMMExclude statement in
the SYSTEM.INI file to exclude the suspect memory
segment.

➤ *Tech tip:* *Start SETUP with /N /I to eliminate automatic
hardware detection. You can then try to manually configure
setup and avoid conflicts.*

Symptom

Windows hangs when loading at the workstation.

Probable Cause

There is not enough memory, there are SYSTEM.INI
conflicts, or there are setup or configuration
problems—that is, there is a conflict between Windows
and Interrupt (IRQ) 2 or 9, the base I/O address 2E0h, and
the EMS page frame D0000-DFFFF and the network board.

Solution

Try to run Windows in any of its three modes: WIN /r (real
mode); WIN /s (standard mode); WIN /3 (386 enhanced
mode). SYSTEM.INI problems will usually prevent
enhanced mode from operating correctly. XMSNET#
problems may be responsible for standard mode
performance failure. Setup and configuration problems
(especially with memory) often result in real mode conflicts.
Change the network board's base I/O address and base
memory address settings. (See Chapter 5, "Workstation
Hardware" for how to resolve network board configuration
conflicts.) You can also use the EMMExclude statement in
the SYSTEM.INI file to exclude the suspect memory
segment.

Symptom

Windows loads into the workstation very slowly after it is installed on the file server, especially when it is running in 386 enhanced mode.

Probable Cause

Swapfiles are being swapped out to a network drive, thus creating more workload for the file server and more traffic on the network. Windows allocates blocks of disk space for the swapfile prior to using it and zero fills the allocated space as a security measure, dramatically slowing access and transmission.

Solution

Move the swapfiles to a local hard disk directory or to a RAM drive.

Symptom

After building application groups, the user ends up with the same application program found in multiple drives.

Probable Cause

The user built application groups by clicking "yes" to the All Drives option but did not use the MAP ROOT command.

Solution

Before entering the SETUP program, map root a drive map for the user to the highest point in the directory tree you, as supervisor, wish the application program to search. Then just select that drive from the dialog box to search applications. Map all other search drives and heavily used regular drive mappings with the MAP ROOT command also, to prevent Windows from resetting them.

> ➤ *Tech tip:* *When you change to MAP ROOT, watch out for applications that have relied on being able to state a complete path based on a previous drive mapping. They will not work correctly after you remap their drive letters with MAP ROOT (see Chapter 1, "System Management," for more details on drive mapping and login scripts).*

Symptom

The user loaded Windows on a 386 workstation and now cannot run applications that previously ran in the 384K upper RAM area.

Probable Cause

The user installed Windows and allowed SETUP to install HIMEM.SYS in the CONFIG.SYS file, disabling any upper-memory managers being used.

Solution

Have the user use Quarterdeck Software's QEMM.SYS version 5.11 memory manager instead of HIMEM.SYS.

> ➤ *Tech tip:* *While you are at the DOS prompt editing your CONFIG.SYS file, also make sure that there is a FILES=60 statement in it and that the SHELL.CFG or NET.CFG file also says FILE HANDLES = 60. Then, make sure that the workstation is running one of the latest shell versions (3.01e or 3.02) and that you have updated the 2.1X utilities, especially BINDFIX and MAKEUSER, with the NetWare Windows utility package or by copying them over from a 2.2 NetWare file server. If the old BINDFIX or MAKEUSER utility is run on a file server logged in to with the new shell, it will not understand the new shell's SHOW DOTS = ON default setting and will cause data loss.*

Symptom

The user receives the error message "Not enough XMS memory to run Windows in standard or enhanced mode."

Probable Cause

The workstation is using the NetWare XMSNET# shell.

Solution

Add more memory to the workstation or use the conventional NET# shell. The workstation should contain a minimum of 4 megabytes of RAM for good performance when two applications are active.

➤ *Tech tip: Always have backup copies of the system.INI and WIN.INI files. These files can become corrupted resulting in Windows' failure. And since they are complex to set up, a backup copy of each one is a safety net worth having.*

Further Help

Microsoft Corporation's "The Windows Resource Kit" is an excellent comprehensive guide for working with Windows 3.0. In addition, Automated Design Systems, Inc. in Atlanta, Georgia, now produces "Windows Workstation," a software product designed specifically to assist in managing and configuring network workstations using Windows 3.0. It is especially useful for its menu, security, and print management features and for permitting a system supervisor to manage and control Windows on a network.

Macintosh Computers

Macintosh computers are becoming increasingly common on NOVELL networks. Since they have a very different operating system than DOS-based PCs, you may need to consult other manuals and guides on their installation and operation if you are not a Macintosh user.

For detailed instructions on Macintosh installations on NOVELL networks, see the NetWare 2.1*X* "Installation Supplement NetWare for Macintosh" and the NetWare 2.2 "Installation and Maintenance for Macintosh" manuals.

Symptom

The Control Panel screen does not display the correct network icon.

Probable Cause

While the Macintosh comes with a built-in Local Talk network driver, you must correctly install the drivers for Ethernet, Token-Ring, or ARCnet.

Solution

Have the user select the INSTALLER program in the Utilities folder to place the correct driver on the Macintosh. Then, have the user select the network control device (CDEV) from the Control Panel to choose the correct network topology.

Symptom

The file server name does not appear in the Chooser window or the user cannot log in to the file server.

Probable Cause

The user did not make the network driver active by clicking it, the user did not double-click the name of the file server, or the user created a user password more than eight characters long (the maximum password length for a Macintosh).

Solution

Have the user make sure the Active button for the chosen
network is darkened in the workstation's Chooser window.
Have the user click it if it is not, then double-click the
name of the file server. Check the length of the user's
password name by logging in as supervisor on a DOS
workstation and running SYSCON. Select User Information,
the user's name, and Change Password to type in a
password eight or fewer characters in length.

Further Help

See the *NetWare Workstation Troubleshooting and
Maintenance Handbook* by Edward Liebing, Charles D.
Knutson, and Michael Day (LAN TIMES/McGraw-Hill,
1990) for detailed instructions on setting up and logging in
to a Macintosh.

5

Workstation Hardware

No matter how well the workstation operating system, routing, and shell files have been loaded and configured, unless the hardware itself is receiving clean power and is built of serviceable components, the workstation will not be reliable.

The workstation is made up of a number of critical components, including a power supply, one or two floppy drives, possibly a hard drive, random-access memory (RAM) chips, a system board, control cards, a monitor, and a keyboard. If any one of these components becomes unreliable or completely fails, users will experience problems ranging from intermittent errors to an inability to access the network or even to boot up the workstation. If you have limited experience with hardware, you may be better off having the workstation tested by a professional technician. However, there are a number of relatively simple preventive steps you can take and diagnostic techniques you can implement if users do experience workstation problems.

As you use this chapter to guide you in checking workstation hardware, keep in mind a few do's and don'ts. Do make sure the workstation is plugged into a good working AC power outlet that has good ground and is properly wired. (You can buy an inexpensive $5-$10 circuit tester or wall outlet analyzer at any hardware store to test the outlet.) Make sure all cable and power connections are tightly plugged in. Check for obvious errors such as proper adjustment of the brightness or contrast control if the monitor does not light up or looks fuzzy. Make sure all drive and power indicator lights come on when they should. Listen for any abnormal sounds coming from the hard drive or power supply that may indicate bearings are wearing out or overheating. Finally, remember that substitution is a very simple diagnostic routine used by most technicians and that you can also use it to isolate problems to the component level. However, if you do swap known working parts for suspected faulty parts, be careful always to turn off workstation power before you unplug or plug in any components; if you don't, you could seriously damage the parts or the workstation. Also, if you remove control cards from their slots in the workstation, place them inside the anti-static bags they were shipped in if you have them, or lay them down on a piece of aluminum foil, to protect them from damaging levels of static electricity that can exist on table surfaces or on your body.

In fact, you should not work inside the workstation at all unless you are wearing an anti-static wrist strap that grounds you to the case of the workstation. (These wrist straps can be purchased for $15-$25 at any good electronics store.) The workstation should then be plugged into a grounded outlet. This earth ground prevents your body from potentially discharging thousands of volts of static electricity into the five volt chips on the system board or control cards. Professional anti-static wrist straps also have protective resistors built into them to prevent you from being shocked by any potential flaw in the workstation's wiring or circuitry.

Do not take apart and work inside the power supply or monitors on workstations. These devices contain very high voltage levels that can cause serious injury if you handle them incorrectly. Do not handle floppy drives or hard drives roughly. Treat them very gently if you remove them from the workstation and place them carefully on anti-static foam to avoid jarring the read/write heads and exposing the drive circuitry to static electricity. And most important of all, make absolutely sure you have a complete, current,

verified backup of all data before you work on any
workstation hard drive or floppy disk problem.

If you take these simple precautions and use this chapter
as a diagnostic guide, you can successfully troubleshoot
many common workstation problems.

Power

Clean power is an absolute necessity for proper
workstation and network performance. Blackouts,
brownouts, voltage spikes, or noise cause workstation
failure and possible data loss.

Blackouts and brownouts occur when power fails as a
result of storms or electric company power-generation
problems. Obviously, you will lose data that has not been
saved to the local workstation hard or floppy disk or to the
file server if AC power suddenly disappears or drops below
the voltage level needed to keep the power supply in the
workstation functioning properly. Voltage spikes and noise
can result from electric company power fluctuations or
from having equipment such as copier machines or space
heaters plugged into the same circuit as the workstation.
These intermittent power pulses can interfere with data
transmission and program operation at the workstation and
can also result in data loss.

Symptom

Insufficient voltage or noise on the line, causing IPX or
shell disconnects, results in a "Network error sending (or
receiving) on the network" message. Application programs
fail, resulting in data loss or database file corruption.

Probable Cause

The workstation is not plugged into an uninterruptible power supply (UPS) or line filter. It is plugged into a cheap surge suppressor designed to prevent high voltage spikes from damaging equipment but not designed to prevent brownouts or line noise.

Solution

Purchase a line-conditioning unit ($75-$125). This device filters line noise and provides constant clean AC power to the workstation at correct voltage levels. If you can afford the extra money ($150-$400), a UPS is the best protection. A good UPS provides battery power to the workstation for 10 or 15 minutes when AC power is lost, giving you time to save your work to the file server. Many UPSs also provide line noise filtering and power conditioning. (See the section "AC Power and UPS Monitoring" at the end of Chapter 3 for a more complete discussion of the different types of UPSs.)

Symptom

The entire network experiences intermittent transmission problems or complete failure.

Probable Cause

An improperly conditioned power outlet at one workstation places voltage on the network cabling through that workstation's network board connection. Poor or no ground wires at the wall outlet render the surge suppressor useless and cause looping or floating ground conditions.

Solution

Purchase a circuit tester at any hardware store to check your wall outlet for correctly wired hot, neutral, and ground lines. Or use a digital volt-ohm meter to test the AC voltage at the wall outlet. You can also use a power monitor at the outlet to reveal changes in voltage over time. This device can indicate if, for instance, a photocopy machine motor comes on line and causes a power surge at a particular time of day (see the Appendix, "Useful Hardware Tools").

Further Help

Call a professional cabling or electrical company to test all AC, hot, neutral, and ground lines. Corrective action can then be taken at the exterior power service entrance or at an interior circuit breaker box.

If problems persist, you may have a failing internal power supply. On some machines, such as Compaq, Wyse, Hewlett-Packard, and IBM PS/2, the internal power supplies are built with a proprietary design and are relatively expensive to replace. It may be worthwhile to take the machine to a qualified dealer or reseller to have the power supply repaired.

The power supply is an inexpensive item for many clones and compatibles ($100-$200, depending on voltage output). Replace it.

RAM

Without sufficient and reliable memory, a workstation is severely hampered. Today, more than ever before, there is an increasing demand for large amounts of fast random-access memory (RAM) to service the increasingly powerful application programs on the market.

RAM chips are made by many different manufacturers but are sold in two basic packaging types—the older dual in-line pin (DIP) chips that are plugged into individual sockets, or the modern single in-line memory modules (SIMMs) that are made up of a bank of chips soldered onto one modular board that clips into place. DIP-style RAM chips are best removed with an inexpensive integrated circuit (IC) puller available for less than five dollars at most electronics stores. They can be installed in their sockets by hand. (Always be careful not to bend or crimp the pins as you plug the chips in since they are difficult to straighten and easy to break). SIMM modules can be removed and installed with your fingers and possibly a small screwdriver since they are held in place by small spring clips easily bent back with a fingernail or thin screwdriver blade. Make sure they seat securely in their holders and are clipped all the way in when you install them. Always wear an anti-static wrist strap when you handle, remove, or install RAM chips.

Symptom

"Parity error" messages appear, the workstation locks up, or it hangs.

Probable Cause

There are power glitches, corrupt program files, static electricity discharges, mixed timing in the RAM chips, or poorly seated RAM chips.

Solution

Most of the time, parity errors are transient and can be cleared by rebooting the machine. You will lose data in RAM not yet saved to the file server and may corrupt a program or database file. Using a static-free spray on carpets and providing anti-static mats or keyboard pads also helps prevent parity errors from occurring.

If rebooting does not clear the error and you have recently added more RAM to the workstation, you may have mixed chips with different speed ratings or made by different manufacturers. Try to make sure the chips are all made by the same manufacturer and are rated at the same nanosecond rating. (The number appears on the chip, that is, a -70 is 70 nanoseconds, or 70 billionths of a second, access time. The access time is how long it takes the central processing unit (CPU) to read data from memory. The lower the number, the faster the chip.)

Before you replace suspected bad chips, push down on the dual in-line pin type of chips to make sure they are well seated (they can work themselves loose over time). Reseat single in-line memory modules (SIMMs) by loosening the clips holding them in on each side, pulling each bank out, and then reinstalling and reseating them. (During these procedures, wear an anti-static wrist strap to discharge any static buildup in your body.) Reseating often fixes intermittent problems or parity errors.

Further Help

If the parity errors continue, perform a lengthy test of the RAM chips with a program such as CheckIt and replace the faulty chips. Or simply replace the chips one bank at a time until the problem disappears. If you replace all the RAM chips and the workstation continues to produce error messages, you need professional service on the workstation.

Symptom

The user receives the error message "Cannot set path for file."

Probable Cause

A RAM error destroyed the shell's drive table.

Solution

Reboot and reload the shell at the workstation. If the error persists, test the workstation RAM with CheckIt and replace bad RAM chips as indicated.

Symptom

Database files are corrupted because the workstation fails in the middle of a database transaction. All users are locked out of the database or get critical error messages while running the database program.

Probable Cause

An incomplete database transaction occurs, caused by sudden workstation disconnects resulting from power supply or RAM failure.

Solution

Flag your large database data files with the T flag. For example: "FLAG Yourfile.dbf /T." This marks the file so that NetWare 2.2's transaction tracking system (TTS) "rolls back" the incomplete transaction and returns the database file to its original condition. The database is not corrupted, and other users can work. (TTS is also available in NetWare 2.1X if you have the system fault tolerant [SFT] version).

➤ Tech tip: This may not be a good idea for some database program files. dBASE files are especially susceptible to damage when you use transaction tracking. Check with the program developer before using the T flag.

Floppy and Hard Drives

If you cannot boot from the floppy drive or hard disk, the workstation is useless. You must have reliable access to the magnetic storage media at all times, especially as hard drives become more critical to workstation performance for programs like Windows 3.0 and OS/2.

Floppy and hard drives are connected to most workstations' power supplies with a four-pin power cable and to the control card by a flat-ribbon signal cable. These cables should always be securely plugged into their connectors and should not be crimped or damaged. The drives are then held in place in most computers by slide mounts and small screw brackets. IBM (in PS/2s) and some other manufacturers install their drives so that they plug directly into control cards without the use of cables and are held in place by special tension mounting brackets or clips.

Keep in mind that there are four different floppy drive formats in use today—360 kilobyte and 1.2 megabyte formats for 5 1/4-inch drives and 720 kilobyte and 1.44 megabyte formats for 3 1/2-inch drives. And note that IBM has just announced a 2.88 megabyte floppy drive format for 3 1/2-inch drives that promises to become a new standard. The formats are all downwardly compatible only—that is, you can read a 360K floppy disk in a 1.2MB floppy drive, or a 720K floppy disk in a 1.44MB floppy drive, but you cannot read the higher capacity floppy disks in the lower capacity drives.

Also note that there are several different types of hard drives available today for 286, 386, and 486 workstations. The oldest and still most widely used is called the ST506/412. Drives in this category work with any standard AT hard drive controller. The head and cylinder count of the hard drive is keyed to the basic input output system (BIOS) drive type table, which you access on the workstation by running the SETUP program built into the workstation or supplied by the manufacturer on floppy disk. (IBM calls this the Reference Disk for their PS/2 computers.) The information in this setup area of memory is maintained by a battery during periods when the workstation is powered off. As long as you have a drive that matches the head and cylinder count of a drive type identified by running SETUP, you can use the hard drive in the workstation.

The enhanced small systems device interface (ESDI) is another type of hard drive; it is two to three times faster than and can store five to ten times more data than the older ST506/412 drive. ESDI drives are also more intelligent drives than the ST506/412 type and can be programmed at the time of installation with a head and cylinder count that does not have to match what is available in the setup area of the workstation. ESDI drives, however, require a special ESDI controller.

Small computer systems interface (SCSI) hard drives are built to be totally self sufficient and require no identification by the setup program in the workstation. Like ESDI drives, they are very fast and capable of large amounts of data storage. SCSI drives can also be daisy-chained so that as many as eight drives can operate from one SCSI controller. (ST506/412 and ESDI drive controllers are generally limited to two drives.)

Finally, intelligent drive interfaces, labeled either IDE or IDA, are fast becoming popular. These drives use proprietary interfaces developed by each manufacturer, so they are generally not interchangeable with another manufacturer's controller. They are, however, cheaper and as fast as ESDI or SCSI drives, although they do not have the storage capacity of those drives.

Before you attempt to troubleshoot floppy or hard drive problems, make sure you know which type of drive you have since the solutions differ for different drives. And be especially careful to always have an up-to-date, verified backup of the entire hard disk before you attempt any diagnostic procedures on a hard drive.

Symptom

The user receives a "601" error message when the workstation boots, and the floppy drive fails to load the workstation boot files.

Probable Cause

There is a broken cable, failed controller, or floppy drive with a speed, alignment, or electronic problem.

Solution

Cables, controllers, and floppy drives are inexpensive components. It is best to simply replace failed components rather than try to have them repaired.

Symptom

The user receives no error message but still cannot boot the workstation with a known good working boot disk in the floppy drive.

Probable Cause

The user is using a high-density disk in a low-density drive or the CMOS setup has lost its configuration information.

Solution

Check to make sure the user is not trying to use a high-density disk in a low-density drive (that is, a 1.2 megabyte disk in a 360K 5 1/4-inch drive or a 1.44 megabyte disk in a 720K 3 1/2-inch drive). This can easily happen if users switch boot disks from workstation to workstation. Next, run the SETUP program on the workstation and make sure the floppy drives are identified correctly. To run SETUP, simply reboot the machine and either follow the screen prompts (most clones have you press either the DEL key or the CTRL-ALT-ESC key sequence during the boot cycle) or use the setup disk shipped with the computer (Compaq, IBM, Hewlett-Packard, and others).

Symptom

The user receives a "17XX" error message on workstation bootup.

Probable Cause

The hard drive cable, controller, or hard drive unit at the workstation has failed physically, or there is the wrong hard drive configuration in the CMOS setup.

Solution

Setup problems are the easiest to fix. Make sure the drive type in the setup matches the hard drive head and cylinder count for ST506/412 drives.

If the drive works again but it fails every time after you power off and on, the batteries in the workstation that maintain the CMOS setup information have died. Once you replace them and rerun SETUP, you should have no further problems.

Further Help

If you are not sure how to find the correct drive type or if you are using an ESDI or SCSI drive, you may need to call the hard drive or controller manufacturer's technical support line for assistance.

➤ *Tech tip: Many ESDI drives use a drive type of 1, and the BIOS ROM on the hard drive controller then overwrites the computer CMOS information with its own "translation" of the hard drive head and cylinder count. SCSI drives usually require the hard drive type to be set to NONE since they assume all control over drive operations internally.*

Symptom

Changing setup fails to fix the problem and the user continues to get "1701" error messages.

Probable Cause

The hard drive cable or controller has failed.

Solution

Replace the hard drive cable and reboot. If the error message still appears, replace the controller with one of exactly the same make and model.

Further Help

If the workstation continues to have problems, you need to have the hard drive checked by a professional service technician.

➤ *Tech tip: Of course, you have the regular full backup you have been making on a daily basis to restore all the valuable information the user stored on the hard drive, right?*

Symptom

The user does not get "17XX" error messages or DOS error messages, but the hard drive still fails to boot.

Probable Cause

The active partition on the hard drive is lost or the partition drivers do not load correctly from the CONFIG.SYS file.

Solution

Run FDISK and check to make sure that the drive is still partitioned correctly and that the first partition is marked active (see your DOS manual for this procedure). Check that device drivers such as Ontrack System's Disk Manager DMDRVR.BIN or Storage Dimensions' Speedstor SSTOR.SYS load correctly from the CONFIG.SYS file with a DEVICE= statement if the hard driver is using these drivers to boot up. Make sure these device drivers are not corrupt and do not conflict with device drivers for programs such as Windows 3.0. As a preventive measure, you can also use Central Point Software's PC Tools Deluxe or Symantec's Norton Utilities to save the partition information on the hard drive so it can be easily replaced if it is lost.

➤ *Tech tip: Rename your CONFIG.SYS file to CONFIG.ORG and reboot. You may get a bootable C drive back again but lose access to other partitions on the hard drive. If this happens, replace the corrupted driver files from the original DISK MANAGER or SPEEDSTOR program disk. Then, rename the CONFIG.ORG file back to CONFIG.SYS and reboot again.*

Symptom

The user can access the workstation hard drive but has occasional boot glitches or other problems.

Probable Cause

There is a corrupt file allocation table (FAT) on the hard drive's first track (track 0).

Solution

Run CHKDSK. If you get a report that there are "Lost clusters in chains" or "Cross-linked files," run CHKDSK/F. This procedure cleans up these misallocated files in the FAT and frees up space on the hard drive. You might also try a third-party utility such as Norton Utilities' Disk Doctor program.

Tech tip: *This is worth repeating: always be sure before you try any hard drive fixes that you have as complete a backup as possible of all your critical programs and data. The file server is usually backed up on a regular schedule, but you may forget about the local hard drive or even make the mistake of thinking data stored there is more protected than the data on the server. This is rarely true.*

Monitors

The functionality of the workstation monitor is critical to the network. The monitor is, after all, the device the user looks at for hours every day. If the images are not sharp and clear, eyestrain can cause headaches and fatigue, which in turn can rapidly wear on nerves. Productivity drops as discomfort increases. Conflicts can also develop between monitor cards and other devices in the workstation. These conflicts can eventually result in a slowdown in workstation processing speed or total workstation failure.

Today, most new workstation color monitors use video graphics array (VGA) technology rather than the older enhanced graphics adapter (EGA) or color graphics adapter (CGA) technology, which do not have as high resolution or offer as many color combinations as VGA. You can easily tell the difference between VGA and the older color monitors since VGA monitors all require a 15-pin connector on the workstation to plug into.

Symptom

The workstation screen image blurs or breaks up into strange characters.

Probable Cause

The monitor needs an adjustment or the monitor or monitor card has failed.

Solution

Check the monitor brightness and contrast adjustments. NetWare's menus or other program's screens may appear blurry or out of focus or you may not be able to see bold highlights because the monitor is not adjusted for the correct background/foreground color combination or the brightness and contrast adjustments are not set properly.

If the problem persists and the monitor or card is under warranty, replace it. If the equipment is out of warranty, don't have it repaired. Given the low cost of most monochrome monitors and cards today, you should simply replace the component with an equal or better part. However, if you have a more expensive VGA monitor, you can usually get it repaired for less than the cost of buying a new one.

Symptom

You upgrade the workstation from monochrome to VGA and now you get "File server not found" or "Error sending (or receiving) on the network" error messages.

Probable Cause

Almost all ARCnet cards are shipped set to a default interrupt request (IRQ) of 2, and other network boards can be and often are set to this IRQ. Unfortunately, many VGA card manufacturers also make use of this IRQ to "cascade" to IRQ 9 on 16-bit cards. This is often not documented anywhere in the VGA card manual. The result is an IRQ conflict that will show up as intermittent workstation hangs or "Error sending (or receiving) on the network" error messages.

Solution

Avoid IRQ 2 on any network board installed in a VGA workstation. If possible, avoid using it all the time. If you have a 16-bit network board, this is usually easy to do since you have the IRQ's 10, 11, 12, 13, and 15 also available (see the next section on network boards).

Network Boards

The network board is the most critical component in workstation performance and reliability. It must be configured correctly to avoid conflicts with other devices in the workstation and to work properly with the software drivers installed on the boot disk. Always read the network board manufacturer's documentation carefully before you install and configure the board itself. Each manufacturer deals with board setup and configuration in a proprietary fashion, and while the general standards governing ARCnet, Ethernet, and Token-Ring protocols are usually adhered to, there are subtle differences that can make or break network performance.

A good rule of thumb is to avoid as much as possible mixing network boards from different manufacturers on the same network. For instance, if you have Thomas Conrad ARCnet cards, try not to mix in Standard Microsystems ARCnet cards. If you have Western Digital Ethernet cards, try not to mix in 3Com Ethernet cards. Even though, theoretically, there should be no problems if you do mix most manufacturers' boards, there is sometimes just enough difference in the various manufacturers' design and compatibility standards to make it, in practice, better to not mix boards if you can avoid it.

Symptom

The user receives a "Cannot initialize LAN card" error message when IPX tries to load, or the NET# shell hangs the workstation as it attempts to load.

Probable Cause

The network board in the workstation is the hardware interface between the IPX protocol driver file you generated in NetWare 2.2 with WSGEN (2.1*X* SHGEN) and the cable connection to the network board in the file server. To operate properly, this board must be set with an interrupt request (IRQ), base I/O address, and base memory address that do not conflict with settings used by other hardware devices installed in the workstation. The network board has a conflict with one or more of these settings.

Solution

Run a program like CheckIt before you install the network board in the workstation to determine which IRQs, base I/O addresses, and base memory addresses are already in use by other hardware devices.

Next, consult the manual shipped with the network board and set the jumpers and dip switches on the board so that you avoid conflicts with those devices. As you do this, make sure you check the network board manual carefully. On most industry standard architecture (ISA) bus network boards, you must move the toggle or slide switches on dual in-line pin (DIP) switches labeled with an SW# to an ON or OFF position to choose a 0 or 1 setting. The combination of those switch settings then identifies the base I/O and base memory address of the board.

➤ *Tech tip:* *Many manufacturers use the ON position to represent a 0 and the OFF position to represent a 1. Check carefully so you do not reverse these settings. Also, jumpers are usually used to set the IRQs on ISA bus network boards. When you move jumpers to set the correct IRQ, make sure you position them over the correct two pins with the metal contact side down.*

On enhanced industry standard architecture (EISA) or micro channel architecture (MCA) bus machines, the network boards are configured using the software reference disk (IBM PS/2s) or a configuration utility. The network boards for these machines are shipped with a serialized disk that you must read in by running the configuration utility. This loads the bus mastering driver for the board. You then choose the IRQ, base I/O address, and base memory address of the board from the configuration setup screen programmed into the BIOS ROM chip in the computer.

➤ *Tech tip:* *Many newer network boards configure themselves automatically for base memory address, DMA channels, and even base I/O address, so you do not have to worry about these settings. However, always be prepared to make sure there are no conflicts with existing hardware.*

Further Help

Read the manual shipped with the network board carefully. Check for special settings such as jumpers to choose between thin or thick cable on Ethernet boards and the time-out period on ARCnet boards. Remember that once you have properly set the board, you must then generate an IPX file that matches the network board's configuration with NetWare 2.2's WSGEN (2.1*X* SHGEN), as discussed in Chapter 4, "Workstation Bootup and NetWare Shell Issues."

Symptom

You have an ARCnet network, and as soon as the user boots up the workstation, both it and another workstation fail or both it and the entire network fail. The user receives

an "Error sending (or receiving) on the network" error
message.

Probable Cause

You must manually set each ARCnet network board to a
unique node address (Ethernet and Token-Ring network
boards are programmed internally with a unique node
address for every board manufactured, so you do not have
to set them manually).

If you set two ARCnet boards to the same node address,
the first one that attaches to the LAN will work, but as
soon as the workstation with the same node address
attempts to attach to the LAN, both workstations will fail.
If the workstation node address is the same as the ARCnet
network board installed in the file server, the entire
network will fail and all workstations will receive network
sending or receiving error messages.

Solution

Log in all users and type **userlist /a**. Write down or use
the PRINT SCREEN key to print the hexadecimal addresses for
all the workstations that appear. Set the network board you
are installing to a unique node address that does not
conflict with any already assigned workstation node
address. Remember, these addresses appear in
hexadecimal so you must set the switches as two groups
of four. For instance, if you want to set the address to 8A
hex, you should set the switches to 10001010.

➤ *Tech tip: Reserve 1 through F hex (which is 1 through 15
decimal) for the file servers on your network. Start
workstations with 10 HEX (16 decimal). This helps to avoid
future conflicts between the file server and a workstation.
Never set an ARCnet card to the node address of 0—it will
not work at all!*

Maintain a database of workstation numbers and node addresses to help you prevent conflicts in the future. Such a database does not require a lot of work to maintain and should become part of your network documentation.

Symptom

You set up the workstation for remote boot using DOSGEN correctly (see Chapter 4, "Workstation Bootup and NetWare Shell Issues") but the workstation still cannot attach to the file server.

Probable Cause

You forgot to install the remote boot prom in the network board, or after you installed it you did not set the jumpers correctly or you installed the prom backward.

Solution

The remote boot jumper must be either removed or shifted to enable the card to see the remote boot prom, which you should have plugged into the socket on the network board. The prom must also be installed correctly. Usually you will find a notch or small circle on one end of the chip that keys to a notch on the socket the chip plugs into. Make sure you line up the notched ends correctly. Read the manual that comes with the network board for detailed instructions.

Symptom

On a twisted-pair ARCnet network, all jumpers and switches are set correctly on the network board, but users still receive "Error sending (or receiving) on the network" error messages on one or more workstations.

Probable Cause

The terminator is missing in the open twisted-pair connector on the back of the board, or the board is not cabled in a daisy chain to another board.

Solution

On twisted-pair ARCnet cards, you must either have a terminator plugged into the open twisted-pair connector on the network board or plug in a twisted-pair cable that goes to another ARCnet twisted-pair board. The last board in such a daisy chain must be terminated. These terminators are usually shipped with the card but can be purchased separately.

Further Help

Some ARCnet boards have jumpers that allow them to be configured as either twisted-pair or coaxial boards or in a star or linear bus configuration. Read the manual that comes with the card to choose the correct setting.

Symptom

The user receives an error message "Cannot initialize LAN card" or "A file server cannot be found," the workstation hangs, or all workstations receive "Network error sending (or receiving) on the network."

Probable Cause

BNC connectors, twisted-pair plugs, or Token-Ring adapter or patch cable connectors are not securely twisted on all the way or plugged in firmly. On thin Ethernet or ARCnet linear bus networks, a faulty network board connection can stop all workstation communications along the trunk until the problem is corrected. The same problem can occur on daisy-chained ARCnet networks.

Solution

Tighten all BNC conectors securely, twisting clockwise until they seat in the special groove. Unplug twisted-pair connectors and plug them in again until you hear a distinct snap as they seat in place. Make sure the screws are tight on the Token-Ring AUI connector or the thick Ethernet AUI drop cable connector that attaches to the back of the board.

Symptom

IPX returns an error message at the workstation that it cannot "Initialize the LAN card" or "Cannot find the LAN card," and all IRQ, base I/O, and base memory address settings are correct.

Probable Cause

The network board has failed.

Solution

Network board manufacturers usually ship a test utility you can run on their board after it is installed in the workstation and before you try to load IPX or NET#. If IPX or NET# fails to connect the workstation to the LAN, and if you have made all of the checks for avoiding conflicts, selecting the correct IPX configuration option and ensuring that connections are tight, run the board manufacturer's test utility. You may simply have a bad board that needs to be replaced. If you do not have a test utility, replace the board and try to load IPX again.

Symptom

The user receives the error message "No free connection slots available" when the workstation attempts to load Net#.

Probable Cause

Users have used up all the available login connections on the file server or there is a bad card on one workstation broadcasting corrupt information.

Solution

If possible, type userlist /a at a workstation already logged in to the network to make sure users have not exceeded the number of logical connections provided by the version and level of NetWare you are using. In 2.1*X* versions of NetWare, ELS level I allows 4 connections, ELS level II allows 8, and Advanced and SFT NetWare allow 100. In 2.2 NetWare, you have a choice of a 5-, 10-, 50-, or 100-connection version.

➤ *Tech tip: NetWare logical connections are also used for adding programs such as value added processes (VAPs) and value added device drivers (VADDs), to the file server. Thus, you might have a 100-user version of NetWare but only be able to log in 90-plus users before running out of connection slots. This problem was addressed in some of the very latest releases of 2.15c and in all 2.2 NetWare versions by increasing the number of logical connections available for such devices. For instance, if you run FCONSOLE and look at the statistics Summary screen in the 50-user version of 2.2 NetWare, you will find you have 66 logical connection slots available, although only 50 connections can actually be used to log in users. If the problem persists and you have not exceeded the logical user limit, log out and power off all workstations. Boot them onto the network one at a time.*

If you get the error message as soon as a particular workstation boots up, replace the network board in that workstation.

Keyboards

The user cannot use the workstation without a working keyboard. This device takes all of the pounding and punishment the sometimes frustrated user can provide. Keyboards are amazingly durable for the most part, but they can and do fail over time.

Symptom

The user receives a "301" error or KB (keyboard error) message.

Probable Cause

The switch on the back of the keyboard is set to XT instead of AT, or vice versa. The cable on the keyboard is not plugged in or has come loose. The keyboard is bad. The keyboard chip on the system board is bad. The keyboard ROM is bad.

Solution

Set the keyboard switch correctly. Check the keyboard connector to make sure it is tight—pull it out, plug it back in, and restart the workstation from power OFF/ON. Replace the keyboard with a known working keyboard. Turn off the power, open the cover of the computer, and locate a socketed chip near the keyboard plug. Ground yourself using an anti-static wrist strap and then push down on the chip to reseat it. Power on again.

Further Help

If the problem persists, contact your hardware vendor for a BIOS ROM/keyboard chip replacement set or a system board replacement.

Macintosh Computers

Many PC workstation hardware problems already discussed also apply to Macintosh computers. These machines are just as susceptible as PCs to power, cabling, RAM, and connectivity problems. A few of the most common problems peculiar to the Macintosh are listed in this section. For more detailed information, see the NOVELL "Macintosh Installation" supplement you received when you purchased your NetWare for Macintosh kit and the *NetWare Workstation Troubleshooting and Maintenance Handbook* by Edward Liebing, Charles D. Knutson, and Michael Day (LAN TIMES/McGraw-Hill, 1990), which provides more detailed background information on the Macintosh.

Symptom

The user cannot mount the volume and get the "Welcome to Macintosh" dialog box when he or she boots up. The workstation hangs.

Probable Cause

The workstation has a corrupt file system on the boot volume of the hard disk, possibly caused by power spikes, RAM problems, or hard disk failure.

Solution

Boot from a floppy disk with a known good System and Finder. As you boot, hold down the OPTION and COMMAND keys. The Macintosh operating system will attempt to rebuild the files needed to boot the system.

If this does not fix the volume, run the Apple Disk First Aid program. If the problem persists, reinstall the hard disk driver shipped with the hard drive.

If problems still persist, you may try a utility such as the Symantec Utilities for Macintosh to either repair the drive or recover the data on the volume.

If all else fails, take the Macintosh to an authorized dealer for repair or replacement of the hard drive or power supply.

Symptom

Part or all of the "Welcome to Macintosh" dialog box displays, but the workstation hangs. Or the dialog box informs the user that it cannot load the Finder program or that it is not valid.

Probable Cause

The user added a desk accessory or font that corrupted the operating system. This probably occurred because the hard disk is heavily fragmented, causing the system files to be spread over the surface of the hard drive, and one area containing those files is corrupt.

Solution

Reboot the workstation from a floppy disk and run the Symantec Utilities for the Macintosh defragmentation utility. Then run the Installer and reinstall the System and Finder programs.

Symptom

The user's application fails to execute and a "Not enough memory" error message appears on the screen even though there is enough memory in the machine.

Probable Cause

RAM in the Macintosh has become fragmented as a result of continual opening and closing of applications or opening NetWare volumes with hundreds of files or folders while the MultiFinder program is active. Finder has limited RAM allocated to open and display NetWare directories.

Solution

Use Finder to increase the actual allocated size of memory in the Get Info window and then reboot the Macintosh.

Symptom

The "Welcome to Macintosh" dialog box displays and goes away, and booting proceeds normally but suddenly freezes.

Probable Cause

An INIT program linked into the operating system is corrupt.

Solution

Reboot the Macintosh from a floppy disk and remove the furthest right INIT icon by dragging it to the root level. If you can reboot successfully, you have identified the offending INIT.

➤   *Tech tip: Try renaming the bad INIT and replacing it in the System folder so it reloads in a different order.*

If you still cannot boot, remove all INITs from the System Folder, and then replace them one at a time and reboot after each replacement until you isolate the corrupt INIT.

Symptom

The Macintosh attempts to mount a NetWare volume but returns an error message like "The volume is damaged" and then does not mount the volume.

Probable Cause

The user does not have sufficient rights in the DESKTOP directory located at the root level of the NetWare for Macintosh volume. There are four critical files in this directory that must be accessed for the volume to mount.

Solution

Grant Read, Filescan (NetWare 2.1*X* Open and Search), Write, Create, and Delete rights to Macintosh users in this directory. Use Syscon to create a group with these trustee rights for all Macintosh users and make the users members of this group.

6

Cabling

Many LAN problems relate to the network cabling system. To avoid these problems, you must properly run the cable and install connectors; you must assemble, test, and connect concentrators, hubs, and multiple access units (MAUs); you must properly terminate cable ends, passive hubs, and cards; you must avoid sharp bends and proximity to high-level noise or power sources; and you must not exceed distance limitations or cable specifications.

This chapter discusses common cabling and connectivity problems. For complicated installations, you may need to use sophisticated tools and techniques beyond the scope of this book. To assist you, a brief description of some of these tools and their uses is included in the Appendix, "Useful Hardware Tools." If you are working with a very complex network, you should consult a professional network cabling company.

Detailed specifications for the three most popular cabling systems used with NetWare—Ethernet, ARCnet, and Token-Ring—can be found in the NetWare 2.2 "Installation Supplement" manual and the NetWare 2.1X "Supplement" guides. These guides, however, address only the most generic implementations of these cabling systems. Today, there is a wide range of manufacturers and products. You must consult the manuals shipped with the product to ensure you have accurate specifications and do not violate that particular product's limitations or configuration rules.

This chapter begins with a brief description of COMCHECK and NETWARE CARE. The chapter then goes on to discuss cabling problems in the context of the three major communication protocol standards: Ethernet, ARCnet, and Token-Ring. In each case, where appropriate, the problems are further categorized by whether they affect one workstation, several workstations, or all workstations on the network.

NOVELL Diagnostic Software Utilities

COMCHECK and NETWARE CARE are two very useful software utilities for testing cable transmission problems. COMCHECK is shipped free with NetWare. NETWARE CARE is sold by NOVELL as an additional diagnostic utility.

COMCHECK

For any suspected cabling problem on either a new or existing installation, when more than one workstation is involved, the NOVELL utility program COMCHECK, which can be found on the NetWare 2.2 WSGEN disk or 2.1X DIAGNOSTICS disk, is an excellent troubleshooting tool.

To use COMCHECK, type **down** at the file server and turn the power off. Load IPX in each workstation and run COMCHECK each time after you load IPX. Give each workstation a unique name or number when COMCHECK requests it. The name and node address of all workstations that have successfully attached to the wire will appear in the COMCHECK screen of each workstation. If nothing appears in the screen when you run COMCHECK, the workstation board or IPX may be faulty (see Chapter 4, "Workstation Bootup and NetWare Shell Issues," or Chapter 5, "Workstation Hardware"). If a workstation name and node address are displayed in bold or a highlighted color, the connection to that particular workstation has failed.

NETWARE CARE

NETWARE CARE must be purchased separately from NOVELL. It provides information on such statistics as packet transmits and receives, collisions, and errors. These statistics may then be graphed for analysis. You can test cable segments by doing a point-to-point test to identify bad connections, communication problems, and overloads. The list price on this product is $195 for the Level I product. However, you should check with a NOVELL reseller for current pricing.

Ethernet

The most popular cabling system for Ethernet's linear bus protocol is the 10-megabit/second Thin Net coaxial cable system. This system is relatively inexpensive and easy to install. You daisy-chain the cable from one workstation to another by directly connecting to the BNC T-connectors on each workstation network board. The cable is rated as RG58A/U and utilizes 50-ohm terminating resistors on each end. BNC connectors are crimped onto the end of the coaxial cable by using a special crimping tool. BNC connectors used for network cabling are very similar to BNC connectors used to hook up cable television cabling. However, instead of a screw connection, network BNC connectors must be securely twisted onto the male end of a T-connector on an Ethernet system, which in turn must be securely twisted onto the male stub of the network board. All BNC connectors have a brass or copper pin in the center that is crimped onto the core signal wire that passes through the center of the cable from end to end.

Twisted-pair cabling is being used increasingly for Ethernet networks that adhere to the new 10Base-T standard. This cabling system requires a Concentrator device to which all twisted-pair lines from the workstations attach. The Concentrator then acts as a central hub for routing network traffic. Twisted-pair connectors are very similar to the standard phone jack connectors used for telephones. However, since the cabling is used for data transmission rather than voice transmission, twisted-pair cabling must have at least two twists per foot, and the connector ends must be properly installed and terminated.

Symptom

A "File server not found" error message appears on booting up the workstation. "Network error sending (or receiving) on the network" messages appear. No other workstation on the LAN is having problems.

Probable Cause

The T-connector is loose, disconnected, or has failed.

Solution

Twist the BNC end on the T-connector that attaches to the network board and make sure it snaps in securely. If problems continue, replace it with a new T-connector.

➤ *Tech tip: Replacing the T-connector requires disconnecting both ends of the linear bus, thus stopping all network traffic. Make sure all other workstations on the network are logged out before you break the bus.*

Symptom

A "File server not found" error message appears on booting up the workstation. "Network error sending (or receiving) on the network" messages appear. All other workstations on the LAN are having problems.

Probable Cause

A BNC connector attached to a T-connector is loose or has been disconnected, or the wire inside is broken. One or both terminators are loose or have been removed from the ends of the linear bus. A cable run between workstations is bad.

Solution

Tighten all BNC connectors and terminators securely. Make sure terminators are in place and are the correct type and impedance. If the problem continues and the cable segments are short and easily accessible, you can disconnect segments one at a time and test the network by using a deductive method. Start by logging out all users from the network. Then, begin at one end of the linear bus and terminate the cable before it connects to the last workstation. Use COMCHECK as described in the previous section, "NOVELL Diagnostic Software Utilities," or attempt to log in to the file server. Work your way back up the bus from workstation to workstation until you have isolated the faulty connector or cable run. If the cable segments are lengthy or difficult to access, and you have the equipment, use either a DMM or one of the cable-testing tools described in the Appendix, "Useful Hardware Tools." Replace the faulty connector or cable segment once you have it isolated.

➤ *Tech tip: Remember there are probably two sides to the linear bus splitting off from the T-connector at the file server. You may have to perform the isolating procedure on both sides to identify the faulty BNC connector or cable run.*

Symptom

You just added more cable and workstations to the network and now all the workstations are receiving "File server not found" or "Error sending (or receiving) on the network" error messages.

Probable Cause

You either exceeded cabling maximum or minimum distance limitations and segment rules or you did not connect the BNC connectors or terminators properly.

Solution

Double-check your BNC connectors and terminators. Make sure you are within the guidelines for Thin Ethernet connectivity: no more than 5 trunk segments on the wire; a maximum segment length of 607 feet (185 meters); a maximum trunk cable length of 3035 feet (925 meters); no more than 30 stations (a repeater counts as one station) connected to one trunk segment; a terminator on each end of each trunk segment; a minimum distance of 1.5 feet (0.5 meters) between T-connectors.

Remember the 5-4-3 rule when you use Ethernet: You can have only 5 segments in series, 4 repeaters, and 3 populated segments attached to PCs. The other 2 segments must remain unpopulated. They are known as inter-repeater links, or IRLs. They contain one repeater at each end and are used to expand the distance covered by the network.

If available, use a time-domain reflectometer (TDR) as described in the Appendix, "Useful Hardware Tools," to measure cable length and test for breaks.

➤ *Tech tip: Thick Ethernet cabling increases the distance limitations of Thin Ethernet through the use of a thicker (0.4-inch diameter) coaxial cable trunk. It can be purchased*

*in precut lengths with connectors installed and requires
N-series terminators at the ends, one of which must be
grounded. Thick Ethernet permits the use of drop cables
from transceivers on the trunk to the workstation's network
board AUI connector. See your NOVELL "Supplement"
manuals and guides for connectivity and distance rules.*

Symptom

On a Thick Ethernet system, "File server cannot be found"
or "Error sending (or receiving) on the network" error
messages appear on one workstation but not on any others.

Probable Cause

The AUI connector is loose or disconnected. The drop
cable is bad. The transceiver is bad.

Solution

Use a small jeweler's screwdriver to tighten the screws on
the AUI connector and seat it securely. If the problem
persists, replace the drop cable and, if necessary, the
transceiver. Remember that replacing the transceiver
requires logging out all users since you will have to break
the trunk segment.

Symptom

"File server cannot be found" or "Error sending (or
receiving) on the network" error messages appear on all
Thick Ethernet workstations.

Probable Cause

There is a bad transceiver or a break in the Thick cable
trunk.

Solution

With all users logged out, replace the transceivers one by one. Use COMCHECK as described in the section, "NOVELL Diagnostic Software Utilities," or attempt to log in to the network after each replacement to isolate the bad transceiver. If the problem persists, use a TDR, or the NOVELL LANalyzer product described in the Appendix, "Useful Hardware Tools," to test the Thick net trunk. If you continue to have problems, call a professional cabling company or consulting firm to check the installation of the Thick cable trunk.

➤ *Tech tip: 10Base-T has become a very popular alternative to Thin and Thick coax-based Ethernet networks since it became an Institute of Electrical and Electronic Engineers (IEEE) 802.3 standard on September 28, 1990. 10Base-T uses unshielded twisted-pair (UTP) wire connected to each workstation from a Concentrator. This "star" implementation of the linear bus transmission protocol makes troubleshooting the bus easier and less intrusive since it is possible to diagnose one workstation's problems without breaking apart the entire trunk. At the same time, 10Base-T maintains 10 megabit/second compatibility with its linear bus cousin and follows the Thin Ethernet 5-4-3 connectivity rule. Most of the less expensive cable testers described in the Appendix, "Useful Hardware Tools," will work for testing 10Base-T cable segments.*

Symptom

"File server cannot be found" or "Error sending (or receiving) on the network" error messages appear on one workstation but not on any others on a 10Base-T network.

Probable Cause

Since all connections are made with wire runs directly from each workstation back to the Concentrator (this is called a "home run"), either the twisted-pair connection at the Concentrator or the network board is bad or the twisted-pair cable run between the two is bad.

Solution

Unplug and plug in the twisted-pair plug several times and try again. If the problem persists, put on a new twisted-pair plug. If the problem still persists, and the cable run is short, run a tested good length of cable from the workstation's network board to the Concentrator, bypassing the suspected cable run. If the cable run is long, use one of the twisted-pair cable testers described in the Appendix, "Useful Hardware Tools," to test the cable. Replace the cable if necessary.

Symptom

"File server cannot be found" or "Error sending (or receiving) on the network" error messages appear on all workstations on a 10Base-T network.

Probable Cause

The twisted-pair cable from the file server to the Concentrator has failed or the Concentrator itself has failed.

Solution

Replace the cable or test it with a cable tester (see the Appendix, "Useful Hardware Tools"). Run COMCHECK or attempt to log in to the file server. If the problem persists, replace the Concentrator.

ARCnet

Star-wired 2.5 megabit/second networks using RG62A/U coaxial cable and 93-ohm terminating resistors with active and passive hubs are the most common configuration for ARCnet, although linear bus and twisted-pair configurations are also popular. ARCnet is a relatively inexpensive and easy-to-install-and-configure wire system. Its maximum cable distance is 20,000 feet, with a 2000-foot maximum distance between active hubs. Recent improvements in ARCnet turbo or enhanced software drivers and turbo network boards have enabled ARCnet to improve its throughput by as much as 100 percent.

➤ *Tech tip: ARCnet linear bus problems have the same error messages as and can be diagnosed just as you would the Ethernet linear bus problems described in the section on Ethernet except that the limitation and configuration rules differ (see your NOVELL "Supplement" manuals for details).*

Symptom

"File server cannot be found" or "Error sending (or receiving) on the network" error messages appear on all workstations on a linear bus network.

Probable Cause

The same potential problems exist for linear bus ARCnet as for linear bus Ethernet—that is, a bad T-connector, a bad cable segment, or a bad BNC connector. In addition, you may have mixed low-impedance star-wired ARCnet network boards, ARCnet network boards jumpered for a star-wired network, or passive hubs into the high-impedance ARCnet linear bus network.

Solution

Use the same troubleshooting techniques as you would for Ethernet linear bus networks, as described in the Ethernet section. In addition, remove any improper boards or passive hubs.

Tech tip: *Star-wired ARCnet systems can be wired with either coaxial cable or twisted-pair cable. Coax uses active and passive hubs for modifying and extending the network. Twisted-pair cable uses active hubs and repeaters. Both systems have special termination rules. Therefore, in addition to the techniques used for diagnosing problems with a 10Base-T Concentrator (described earlier in this chapter in the section "Ethernet"), following are some special considerations for star-wired ARCnet.*

Symptom

"File server cannot be found" or "Error sending (or receiving) on the network" error messages appear on several workstations but not on all workstations on a coax star-wired network.

Probable Cause

The wire connecting one hub back to another hub or the file server has failed, a passive hub has been connected to another passive hub, there are more than 100 feet of cable from one connector on the passive hub to a workstation or another active hub, the passive hub is not properly terminated, or an active or passive hub has failed.

Solution

If the cable run is short and easily accessible, substitute a known good cable for the cable leg you suspect has failed. If the cable run is long or not easily accessible, use a time-domain reflectometer or cable tester as described in the Appendix, "Useful Hardware Tools," to test the cable.

If you continue to have problems, trace the coax back to make sure you did not connect one passive hub directly to another. Make sure you did not exceed the "100-foot radius surrounding any passive hub" connection rule. Make sure each open connector on a coax passive hub is terminated with a 93-ohm terminating resistor. Replace the suspect active or passive hub with a known good working hub.

Symptom

"File server cannot be found" or "Error sending (or receiving) on the network" error messages appear on several workstations but not on all workstations on a twisted-pair star-wired network.

Probable Cause

On a twisted-pair network, the wire connecting one hub back to another hub or the file server has failed; you have exceeded the 400-foot limitation for one wire run from an active hub to a repeater; the last board in the line daisy-chained off the hub or repeater is not properly terminated; or an active hub or repeater has failed.

Solution

Again, if the cable run is short and easily accessible, substitute a known good cable for the cable leg you suspect has failed. If the cable run is long, measure it or use a time-domain reflectometer as described in the Appendix, "Useful Hardware Tools," to check the wire distance from the active hub to the repeater—if it exceeds 400 feet, divide the wire and add another hub or repeater. (Unlike star-wired coax ARCnet passive hubs, star-wired twisted-pair ARCnet repeaters require a power source nearby since they are a signal booster as well as a signal splitter.) If problems persist, check that a terminator is plugged in to the open twisted-pair connector on the last network board in a daisy-chained line. Finally, you may have to replace the suspected hub or repeater with a known working one.

Tech tip: *Never create a "loop." This happens when a cable coming from an active or passive hub passes through other hubs and then connects back into the original hub. Also keep in mind that unlike Ethernet and Token-Ring, all ARCnet cards require that you manually set them to a unique node address (see Chapter 5, "Workstation Hardware"), or you will experience workstation conflicts and network failure.*

Token-Ring

Token-Ring 4/16 megabit/second uses a more complicated and demanding wiring system than either Ethernet or ARCnet. Again, consult the NOVELL "Supplement" manuals for detailed information concerning its configuration and limitations. This section discusses only the small movable IBM Token-Ring system, which uses type 6 shielded twisted-pair cabling and has up to 96 workstations and up to 12 IBM multiple-access units (MAUs or 8228 units). The type 6 cabling uses 8-foot adapter cables to attach from the workstation to a MAU or to a longer (30-, 50-, or 150-foot) patch cable, which acts as an "extension cord."

Each MAU has a ring-in (RI) and ring-out (RO) receptacle in addition to receptacles 1-8 used by the patch or adapter cables. You must use patch cables to attach the RI on one MAU to the RO on another MAU and to attach the RO on the first MAU to the RI on the other MAU, if more than one MAU is used on the network. In other words, the ring must not be broken.

Symptom

The error message "LAN card initialization failed" or
"Cannot initialize LAN card" appears at the workstation.

Probable Cause

In addition to the probable causes defined in Chapter 5,
"Workstation Hardware," on a Token-Ring network the
problem may simply be that the adapter cable is not
plugged in to the network board or the MAU, or the MAU
receptacle is not working. Token-Ring cards must see the
"token" pass at least one time in order to properly initialize.
When this happens, there is an audible click at the MAU,
and IPX loads in.

Solution

Check the adapter cable connector on the card and make
sure the connector is tightly screwed in. Trace the cable to
the MAU or the patch cable and make sure it is properly
plugged in and connected. If the problem persists and you
do not hear a click when IPX loads at the workstation, plug
the adapter cable into a new patch cable or a new
receptacle on the MAU and try again. If you continue to
receive the error, replace the cables and try again. Finally,
replace the network board or, if necessary, the MAU.

➤ *Tech tip: Before you replace the more expensive MAU, use
the special Setup Aid to retest the receptacles. This tool
plugs into a receptacle and lights up briefly. If the light
goes out and you hear a click, you know the receptacle
works.*

Symptom

"File server cannot be found" or "Error sending (or
receiving) on the network" error messages appear on all
workstations on a Token-Ring network.

Probable Cause

One of the MAUs has failed or the adapter and patch cable run from the MAU to the file server has failed.

Solution

Replace the adapter and patch cable run to the file server. If the problem persists, replace each MAU in the ring with a known good working MAU and test after each replacement.

> *Tech tip:* *Patch cables have some special rules you must follow. There are legal restrictions on their use in some areas—check your fire and building codes. They must not be run outdoors or be exposed to temperatures above 167 degrees Fahrenheit or to electric or magnetic interference. They should not be installed in any space used for air handling unless you purchase fire-rated plenum cable. These rules may also apply to coaxial and unshielded twisted pair cable.*

> *Tech tip:* *There are special rules for connecting Token-Ring networks through an IBM Token-Ring network bridge used to link rings together. You must generate software that makes use of a source routing driver for such a cabling system. Consult the NetWare 2.2 "Installation Supplement" manual and the "Installing and Maintaining the Network" manual for more information on source routing with Token-Ring.*

Appendix

Useful Hardware Tools

This appendix is intended to provide brief descriptions of several hardware products useful for diagnosing LAN problems. Software products are not included here since they are described in the text itself where their use applies. Product names and prices mentioned in this appendix are accurate at the time of this writing. However, you should always check with your NetWare dealer, hardware vendor, or electronics store for the most current pricing and availability.

Cable Tester

There are several inexpensive hand-held testers on the market that will detect the most common twisted-pair cabling problems. These devices come with a loop-back plug and scan all pairs on the twisted-pair segment to determine if the cable is shorted or open or has a crossed wire. Most of these testers are in the $100-$300 range, are made by companies such as T&B, MOD-TAP, and MICROTEST, and can be purchased at most electronics supply stores or through mail-order catalogs specializing in electronic test equipment.

Digital Multi-meter

An inexpensive DMM is a very useful diagnostic tool for testing coaxial cable continuity. Digital multi-meters can be purchased at most electronics supply stores and through mail-order catalogs. For computer work, a DMM that can test DC and AC volts, ohms, and AC current accurately should cost between $50 to $100.

The procedure for testing any kind of network coaxial cable with a DMM is as follows. Unplug both ends of the coaxial cable segment you wish to test. Set the meter to the ohms mode. Touch the tip of one of the probes from the DMM—it doesn't matter if it is the red or black probe—to the center pin conductor of the BNC connector on one end of the cable. At the same time, touch the tip of the other probe to the body of the BNC connector. You should get a reading of 1 on the DMM readout window. This indicates there is no continuity between the signal pin and the grounded body of the connector, which is as it should be. If there is any continuity at all—that is, any reading other than 1—then you have a short between the center pin and the ground sheath. Either the BNC connector needs to be replaced or the cable itself has been cracked. This can happen from bending the cable too tightly around corners or stapling it down too hard with unshielded staples.

To test for a break in the cable, use a short jumper clip on one end of the cable to jumper the center pin on the BNC connector to the body of the connector. Go to the other end of the cable and again touch one probe to the center pin and one probe to the body of the BNC connector on that end of the cable. This time, you should get a reading of 0, indicating continuity throughout the cable segment, which is as it should be. If you get a 1 reading here, you have a break in the cable. Again, this usually is the result of bending, stapling, or cutting into the cable.

LANalyzer and LANtern

LANalyzer and LANtern are combination hardware and software products available from NOVELL for sophisticated testing of Ethernet, Token-Ring, and Starlan networks. They are used to determine network activity; provide statistics; and test and monitor performance of file servers, gateways, bridges, and routers. The LANalyzer can also place stress and traffic testing and performance simulation testing on the network cabling system. Together, LANalyzer and LANtern can provide a detailed picture of what is happening on the network if you have considerable expertise with the concepts of packet decoding and protocol analysis. The list price for LANalyzer is approximately $10,000 for either Ethernet or Token-Ring and, for LANtern, approximately $5000. Check with your NOVELL reseller for current pricing.

Power Monitor

A power monitor plugs into an AC receptacle and measures AC power to determine if there are power spikes over a measured period of time. A digital meter can measure voltage levels only at the time it is used. To truly determine if there are problems, voltage levels must be monitored for peaks or lows occurring intermittently over time. Most power monitors are expensive—$3000 or more. One of the best devices on the market under $1000 is made by a company called TLC. Their T1200H product is a power-line monitor specifically designed to measure AC power the way your computer uses it. It requires no programming or adjustments as it captures and displays power-line abnormalities that can affect workstation or file server operation. It can monitor your computer's use of power for up to 24 hours unattended, measuring such abnormalities as high and low voltage, ground faults, high frequency noise, spikes, and dropouts. It lists for $695. TLC Inc., 3034 Scott Blvd., Santa Clara, CA 95054, (408) 986-8300.

Time Domain Reflectometer

The TDR is a more expensive tool for cable testing. Its chief purpose is to measure cable length and detect breaks. The TDR is attached to one end of a cable segment. It then sends out a signal that is reflected back from the other end. The TDR measures the time it takes the signal to get out and back to determine if you exceeded cable length specifications or have a break in the cable. TDRs are relatively expensive devices, in the $1500-$2000 range. They are often incorporated into complete testing devices that also test for attentuation (how much signal loss you have on the cable as a result of noise) and cross-talk. They are made by companies such as STAR-TEK, MICROTEST, and THE BLACK BOX, and can be purchased at most electronics supply stores or through mail-order catalogs specializing in electronic test equipment.

Index

Note: Entries in quotes (" ") are error messages unless otherwise stated.

F

G

H